100 ThiNGs
To HaTE
BefoRE YoU Die

100 Things

To Hate

Before You Die

Claudia Stavola

Unchained Press

To request permissions, contact the publisher at
Unchainedpress@gmail.com

Hardcover: ISBN 978-1-7377715-0-0
Paperback: 978-1-7377715-1-7
Ebook: 978-1-7377715-2-4

FIRST EDITION

Cover design by Laura Duffy
Interior design by Karen Minster
Edited by John Peragine
Cover photograph by Claudia Stavola

Printed by Unchained Press in the USA

claudiacomedy.com

CONTENTS

PART 3

DROPS OF STUPIDER

PART 4

I'M SO OVARY YOU

PART 5
AIN'T THAT A SHAM

PART 6
DOUCHEBAGS, ASSHOLES,
AND OTHER THINGS THAT STINK

PART 7

I BE MIFFED, BOTHERED, AND BEWILDERED

PART 8
JUST GROSS

PART 9
THAT'S NOT ALL SHE WROTE

And Another Thing . . .

INTRODUCTION

I've been in a state of annoyance most of my life. When you think of someone brimming with hate, you probably envision an eighty-seven-year-old lawn-obsessed widower, a chubby guy who only works out his arms, a saliva-spewing televangelist, or a Karen on a plane with her own PA system. You probably wouldn't associate a goofy gal who makes dance videos with her cats with someone who catalogs things she hates in an Excel spreadsheet. If you're wondering what makes me an expert on where to direct your disdain, let me explain.

I grew up so shy that I had no choice but to observe others from the sidelines. Being petite and polite in a family full of boisterous, buxom women made me perfectly content to keep my mouth shut like a yielding 1950s housewife. I was a compact June Cleaver in a family full of opinionated Sofia Vergaras. Imagine the craziest WrestleMania you can think of and add tits to it. That was my family, and I had a front-row seat. Many people might find that entertaining. It was. But it was also angst-inducing for a bashful wuss like me.

Despite the chronic anxiety, something I often heard throughout my life was, "You're always smiling." Well, that and, "Stop crank calling my house! We're not getting back together!" But I was always a jokey, smiley person despite the shyness and social discomfort plaguing me all my life. I was also an old soul in a child's body (now I'm just old in a child's body), so I was more in tune with others' behaviors than a normal kid should've been. That juxtaposition allowed me to develop a healthy balance between empathy and aggravation. It also allowed me to develop buns of steel trying to fight nervous diarrhea on the daily. As a kid, I knew my place, and that was hiding behind the nearest, calmest adult's leg. My reticence was perceived as moodiness. A relative once commented on a photo of me pouting with a giant snarl in my hair, "Look at you, you were always so moody." Of course, I was moody. I was colicky and couldn't get a brush through my hair. And as a young child, I was already agitated by jerky behavior. Whether it was an impatient witch in line at the grocery store or an unmannerly dickhead who hurried to grab a seat on the subway before the elderly passenger could get it, I was always disgusted by people like that.

I learned from my years of observations that most of the things I hate stem from the actions of idiots. As a young kid, I couldn't voice how upset I was over people's shitty behavior. But as I got older, I got bolder. By age ten, I gained the courage to speak up and even dared to push a boy into the bushes at recess after calling my Chinese friend a "chink." I'm not sure if it's a coincidence that age ten was also when I discovered Van Halen and AC/DC. Maybe repeatedly listening to VH's "Atomic Punk" or AC/DC's "Big Balls" every day after school actually gave me some big balls. But from that point on, whenever I witnessed abhorrent behavior, I felt compelled to right the wrong. To me, abhorrent was anything from the woman in TJ Maxx (who I confronted) abusing her daughter, to assholes who don't say thank you when you hold the door for them. That's when an extra loud, "you're welcome!" is in order. When people are rude, mean, or selfish, I feel a fire raging inside me—or is that an untreated hemorrhoid? (Note to self: Contact asshole doctor.) Don't get me wrong. I'm as much of an idiot as anybody else.

But I'm not the inconsiderate, dangerous, always ready to fight for no reason kind. I always have a good reason for nunchucking someone and setting their hair on fire.

There are two types of dummies in this world. The first are the happy, innocent, gentle ones—like the wooden-jewelry-wearing coworker who's renowned for her secret-ingredient seven-layer dip (doesn't that make it an eight-layer dip?). And the other is the uncouth, uninformed, narcissistic ones who refuse to return shopping carts to the cute little corral thingy in the parking lot but group-message bible verses immediately followed by a sassy conspiracy theory meme. Don't you hate that? It's everyday annoyances like tittoos (nope, that's not a typo), delusional confidence, and gender reveal parties that have pushed me to the edge. It's not my fault the world has created an outrageous number of things to aggravate me. Chances are, a lot of these things drive you nuts too.

This is a book that has an alarming number of fart references. It's also a book of essays that dissect—through sarcasm and humor—things that astute people detest. You don't have to read it in any particular order, and you can read it in bed, in class (who am I kidding? Only miserable people over thirty-five are reading this), and when you're acting all nonchalant while tinkling in the corner of the pool. The best part is that nobody's safe. Right, left, up, down, round and round—we all suck, and chances are there's a rant in this book that will explain why. But even though all kinds of people suck, some are more appalling than others. Bertrand Russell once said, "The trouble with the world is that the stupid are cocksure and the intelligent are full of doubt." I have no idea who Bertrand Russell is, but I figured that quote would make me seem bright . . . even though I kept doubting myself (see what I did there?). Also, I chuckled when I saw the word *cocksure*.

If you're questioning your feelings of rage, I can reassure you that you're not crazy for wanting to taser your boss when he makes you apologize to Joyce from finance because she was offended by your "sexist" remark that "all the women in my family are great cooks." I can reaffirm that it's okay to think your best friend is a tightwad for trying to pass off a donation in your name as a gift rather than a figurative turd with a bow on top. And I can assuredly let you know you're a first-class fuckface if you let anything in this book upset you. So put your big-boy pants on—excuse me, I mean, your curvy stretch denim—and enjoy!

PART 1

LOVIN', TOUCHIN', SQUEEZIN', CHEATIN', AND COMPLAININ'

OK STUPid, THeRe ARe PLeNTy Of FisH

WhO DON'T WaNT YoUR DiCK PicS

Every time I turn on the TV, there's a commercial for another dating website. You have Match.com with that dipshit in the hat, daring you to "Come find meeee!" Then there's eHarmony with that creepy old guy. Who the hell's going to him for dating advice? He looks like he couldn't get laid with Bill Cosby's roofies. There's even a site called FarmersOnly.com. Do they really need an app for this? Can't they just follow the smell of manure? Christian Mingle relies heavily on its tagline, "Find God's match for you." Really? God's online? Is he using his high school yearbook picture like the rest of the old farts? "H.A.G.S.! Class of 4 B.C! See you A.D.!" Imagine swiping and seeing God on a cloud in gladiator sandals, feathered hair, and a gauze towel around his waist? There's also a site for Jewish singles called jdate.com, but apparently, membership is very low because they're stuck haggling over the signup fee.

Some dating websites don't need to advertise on TV, such as Grindr and Tinder. They're really just hookup sites, so they're two of the most popular. People know about them through word-of-mouth sores. Grindr is Tinder for gay men. Tinder is popular with heteros. The women using it pretend they're cool with a booty-call, but start incessantly texting their one-night-stand demanding to know his whereabouts. After he blocks her, she creates a fake account on Plenty of Fish to "catch" him in other women's ponds. By the way, could there be a grosser name for a hookup site than one that includes the word *fish*? My favorite is the one for people fifty and older called Our Time. I heard they had to shorten it from the original name because it was way too long. It started out as: Please DearGodDon'tLetMeDieAloneI'mWillingToSettleForAnythingAt ThisPointIdon'tCareIfSheHasAMenopauseMustache.com.

It's incredible how instantaneous everything is now. You just click a button, and poof, you're in a relationship. You don't even have to meet the person or even have a video chat. People refer to a person as their significant other if they've talked online more than two days in a row. Dating and relationships used to be essential decisions that you didn't take lightly. You'd put a lot of thought and effort into finding the person you were going to end up spending the rest of your life resenting. Back in the day, you'd call your girlfriends to go out, dress like a slut, go to the club, meet a guy lurking near the ladies room line, he'd ask you to dance, you held a drink and swayed with your eyes closed, he'd muster up the courage to ask for your number, you went out a few times before he started asking you to chip in for dates, you'd get turned off, you'd begin blowing him off, he'd stalk you at your office, church, and waxing appointments, you'd keep searching for someone better, you couldn't find anyone else (or at least drag home a decent looking heroin addict nodding off in the park), you'd lift the restraining order, and bam, you bagged yourself a husband. That's when we had self-respect.

People say and do things online they'd never normally do in real life. Like if a guy winks and pokes me online, next thing you know, I'm blowing him in the parking lot of a Red Roof Inn.* But if a guy winks and pokes me in real life, first I have to act shocked and appalled . . . before I blow him in the parking lot of a Red Roof Inn. We get so brave behind our electronic devices. Guys send out pictures of their junk like it's a cookie recipe. Newsflash guys: nobody likes crooked cookies. And even if it were symmetrically perfect, what makes you think we want to use it as a screensaver? We don't even want to look at it in real life—that's why we put it in places we can't see it, even when we're using it. I never knew what to do when I got one. Do you want me to review it? *Three out of five stars. Prep time seemed awfully quick. It was a little hard on the outside but soft and mushy on the inside. It left a weird aftertaste. Eat some pineapple next time and skip the asparagus.*

While most of the world is in this electronic sea of dating, there are still some people out there who found love the old-fashioned way (they handed a woman a polaroid of their penis before buying her a drink and plowing her in a Denny's bathroom). When people meet a couple who's been married more than twenty years, they always want to know the secret to a happy marriage. The secret to a happy marriage is secrets ... and permanently deleting your browsing history. You can learn a lot from a person's browsing history. At the beginning of a relationship, you might see your boyfriend's browsing history and notice internet searches for ex-girlfriends. Five years in, you check his history and find searches for redheaded MILFS and babysitter porn. You get to that twenty-year mark, and there are no more searches for exes. There are no more searches for fetish porn. The only searches you find are for 30-gallon drums and the query *Is arsenic detectable in Coke Zero?*

*If you really believe I'm giving blowjobs in the parking lot of a Red Roof Inn to strangers online, you're crazy. Obviously, it's only Marriotts for me. I have some class.

I Have TRUST Issues With YoUR
TOXiC LoVe-LaNGUAGE JaRGON

People whine that relationships are complicated, yet their terminology to describe them is even more complex. I hear these trendy yet superficial words and sayings on reality shows like *Married at First Sight*, *Are You the One?*, and *The Bachelor*. I also see them packaged as "profound" Instagram musings from guidos staring in a gym mirror, or hot chicks in thongs who—for unknown reasons—always look pissed off, pining, or perplexed. If anything, shouldn't they be laughing at the dichotomy of presenting weighty advice while doing something as frivolous as spreading their ass cheeks on a cliff?

Relationship jargon tells you nothing but makes the moron using it believe they revealed everything. Those using the jargon attempt to say things that they think make them sound deep, but they really sound like talking farts. Let's break down some of these gems:

TOXIC: Nobody ever just breaks up anymore. Any relationship that doesn't work out is labeled as toxic. Everything must be depicted as extreme, dramatic, and an unexpected shitshow to the self-proclaimed sufferer. The fact that they met each other in family court awaiting sentencing on domestic abuse charges is never a clue that their relationship might not be filled with rainbows and lollipops. No toxic relationship is complete without a villain who's also known as a gas-lighter and a trigger. The entire relationship revolves around being set off at any moment, and arguing about your previous toxic partners. Despite repeatedly picking assholes (because they're also an asshole), calling it a toxic relationship makes the person sound more like an oblivious victim than an eager volunteer.

I LOVE HARD: This just means you're psycho. The phrase is more familiar with your low-tooth-count 7-Eleven regulars and *Teen Mom* types. Saying you love hard makes the speaker believe they sound passionate and devoted. But what they're really saying is, "I'm an insecure, jealous, paranoid nutjob who pounds my chest while bouncing up and down as I incessantly accuse you of cheating. But it's only because I love hard." Everything has to be at a level ten, no matter how insignificant. Everything fuels their loving hard including your clothing, your holiday office party ("If you sing 'Sleigh Ride' with Brandon from purchasing again, I'll take off all your tires and turn your *car* into a goddamn sleigh because that's how much I fucking love you!"), or your desire to get healthy ("What's with the vegetables and exercising? You know I love you the way you are . . . unable to run away from me or attract anybody else.") If cheating did occur, this idiot inevitably goes psycho on the mistress or paramour rather than the cheater. They don't love hard, but they math hard because they can never put two and two together and realize their poor choices are the problem.

I DON'T WANT TO GET HURT: Stop stating the obvious that applies to every person on the planet. Nobody wants to get hurt. Nobody goes into a relationship hoping to get dumped after finally feeling comfortable enough to wet-fart in front of their significant other.

I DESERVE TO BE TREATED LIKE A QUEEN: Every woman of ripe dating age is convinced she's a queen despite not being a chess piece, a ruler of a monarchy, or a Latifah. And these self-proclaimed queens want everybody to treat them like royalty while treating everyone around them like the help. These broads never resemble or behave like a queen. Queens don't say, "dead ass," "I'll cut you," or "Pass the Grey Poupon. Don't try me, bitch!" There's nothing regal about a beast wearing eyelashes that look like feather dusters, trotting around town in a sports bra, yoga pants, and Ugg slippers with a Starbucks in her claw and a Gucci bag on the crook of her arm, demanding to speak to the manager everywhere she goes before heading back outside to verbally abuse the meter maid for giving her a ticket for unlawfully parking in a handicap spot. The wimpy guys who go along with this should have their balls removed . . . but they can't because they don't have any.

I NEED YOU TO SHOW UP: Showing up used to mean you arrived somewhere. Now it means telling a needy chick everything she wants to hear regardless of how ridiculous. The guy must go overboard with outlandish praise and telling their female temptress whatever she wants to hear as she glares at him with resting-bitch-face until he says the "right" thing (good luck figuring out what the fuck that is). Even when meeting her requirements, she'll never wipe the *I'm one minute away from putting you in timeout again* smirk off her face. The message she sends is, "If you don't tell me everything I want to hear, you're not getting any of this recently surgically-rejuvenated-designer-vagina."

TRUST ISSUES: This one is code for, "I've made a series of bad decisions picking partners due to my desperation to have a relationship—any relationship—so I really can't trust my own judgment when it comes to finding a mate. Instead of placing the blame on myself where it belongs, I say I have trust issues to make it seem like my previous partners have wronged me in the past while I was an innocent, hapless victim." Banging a guy they just met behind a strip club in a blue Honda Fit while his wife is home alone watching *Bob Hearts Abishola*, ready to give birth, wasn't an indicator that they might have a loser on their hands. Instead, they convince themselves that they're so special that this prize of a man was willing to risk it all to be with them.

CAUGHT FEELINGS: Things you can catch: lice, herpes, fish, a whiff, and Covid-19. Things you can't catch: feelings, a break, and IQ points.

MY RIDE OR DIE: Have you ever noticed Ride or Dies are never married? Wouldn't that be the ultimate gesture of ride or die? But, instead, this sentiment is exclusive to people with pending domestic abuse charges, misspelled tattoos, and a burning discharge emanating from their nether regions.

I PUT UP WALLS: These people say they put walls up to protect themselves from getting hurt, but what they really mean is, "I need to give you porn sex so you'll be addicted to me before you find out how many times I can text you in an hour." The one thing they don't have walls around is their genitals and incessantly talking about all the walls they have up.

I NEED YOU TO LOVE ME FOR WHO I AM: Frankly, I'd rather love you for who Idris Elba is. *I need you to love me for me* is a dumb statement, but I suppose it's necessary when who you really are is someone who kisses your dog on the lips and who believes age is only a number and lives by the credo: "It's not for the law to decide!"

[INSERT NAME] AND I'S RELATIONSHIP: My, my, my. You shouldn't be allowed to reproduce if you say *I's*.

YOU MAKE ME A BETTER PERSON: Isn't there some irony in that statement? If the onus is on somebody else to make you a better person, then how good could the person be who made you better? If they were so great, why would they pick a shithead like you who needs someone else to make them better? Wouldn't they already be attracting someone as decent as they are? I'm pretty sure "You make me a better person" is what guys on death row say to their pen pal wives.

FAIRYTALE ENDING/HAPPY ENDING: If you say the words *fairytale* and *Prince Charming*—and you're not five, or reading to someone who's five—you're a weirdo. Falling in love should be referred to as a happy beginning. Happy endings happen in the backrooms of Asian "nail salons."

MARRIAGE IS WORK: Digging ditches is work. Training for the Olympics is work. Having the right partner isn't a job. If it feels like work and you're not getting paid, it's time to quit.

I'M AFRAID TO BE VULNERABLE: "I'm afraid of my feelings for you," "I'm afraid of being abandoned." "I'm afraid you won't love the real me." *I'm* afraid your constant complaining and overanalyzing is a buzzkill. Do you really need to discuss this crap on a bowling date? Maybe that's why nobody can tolerate you; because the only thing you're not afraid of is being a dud.

LOVE-LANGUAGE: This phrase is another convoluted word-bomb dropped by people who suck at relationships. Maybe they wouldn't suck at them if they didn't overanalyze every little word, sigh, and look. Most guys' love-language is simple: *more shagging; less nagging.* Most women's love-language is: *more pouting; more shouting; if you loved me, you'd know what was wrong; I never want to see you again; why haven't you called me?.* Instead of learning their partner's love-language through quality time spent together, these people would rather complain to friends about their toxic partner, who doesn't show up in their relationship, thus causing trust issues that force them to put up walls.

"I DeSERVe"

Reality dating shows have spawned, or perhaps just shed light on, people who don't do much of anything valuable but believe they deserve a lot in return. It's a mantra I repeatedly hear: "I deserve better! I deserve respect. I deserve to be treated like the queen/king I am."

They abandon any job or responsibility (including children) to go on television to hook up with people they don't even know (I'm being generous suggesting they actually work for a living). They say they're there for love but blow five different guys in a two-day period. Isn't it kind of hard to talk and get to know somebody with the dick-of-the-day in your mouth? And the guys bang everything in sight (including inanimate objects). These people share more bodily fluids than a public toilet. And they deserve respect; why exactly?

Nobody deserves anything they haven't earned! Being a woman doesn't mean we automatically deserve stuff because historically, we've been mistreated in many situations. Do we deserve the same opportunities and pay as men for the same job? Yes (unless you want to drive a bus with more than fourteen passengers in Belarus or polish glass in Argentina). Do we deserve to be treated like Wonder Woman in relationships when we conduct ourselves like Charlie Sheen? Me thinks not. And being male doesn't mean you're owed respect just because you have a penis. You know those guys who think they're being "disrespected" and fly off the handle for dumb shit like getting their name wrong. "Sorry, Victor, for misreading your name as *Victoria* off the attendance list

at the anger management meeting. But was it really necessary to
to shove the guy's glasses down his throat and strike him with his
clipboard?"

The *I deserve* mantra seems to come from people who want to
be treated like something they're not. Instead of working on being
a person who deserves respect and admiration for working hard at
a job, or prioritizing their kids, or advocating for others, they think
they can just bully it out of you by declaring it while practicing
MMA moves on TikTok or twerking on IG. "I have a vagina; therefore, you should worship me no matter how poorly I treat others or
how creepy I look in bikini pics with adult braces."

When a person doesn't respect themselves enough to have standards, how can they believe they deserve someone who actually
does have some? And they always act shocked and devastated when
things don't work out. There's no self-reflection into how their own
behavior—or how expecting quality behavior from an adult male
who wears his pants below his ass cheeks and says things like *bro
code* and *thirst trap*—could've played a role in the shitty outcomes
they keep experiencing. Instead, they deflect and make excuses like
"she ghosted me because she's afraid of how much she loves me" or
"he wants to take things slow" (so slowly that he never answers her
texts after their Tinder hookup). Instead of acknowledging that
shit attracts flies, they blame it on bad luck and being too giving.
How many more himbos and bimbos on reality TV do we need to
see to understand the formula? Himbo and Bimbo sleep together
before knowing anything about each other. *Do her toenails look
like Wolverine claws? Does he wash his dishes with a moldy sponge?
Are his walls decorated with framed magazine clippings about missing women? Has he ever worked as a clown?* One of them inevitably thinks they're in a relationship even when the other is already

onto the next herpes recipient. What woman expects standards from a guy who ate her like sushi at a convenience store? Do these people really think they're going to be sitting in rocking chairs fifty years from now telling their grandkids how they knew it was love at first drunken bang on a pool table while the world watched the whole escapade on MTV?

A decent person with class doesn't need to be told how to treat a partner because they'd already be with one whose behavior warranted it. If a guy's giving out dick samples like he's Baskin-Robbins, he deserves no more respect than the women doing the taste-testing.

———

Dear Reality Stars,
Keep complaining and acting like dramatic wackos and wonder how that's not appealing and deserving of better, or conducive to being a "queen" or "king".
*I'll keep watching because I **deserve** a good laugh.*

HONey, I ShRUNK My BaLLs

Married guys making plans in 1977:

FRANK: Wanna grab a beer tomorrow? Cubs are playing.

DICK: See you at noon.

Married guys making plans in 2022:

KYLE: Do you think you can scoot out for a bit tomorrow
to watch the Sox?

TRAVIS: Ooh, that might be tough. Megan gave me a honey-
do list that I gotta bang out before the weekend's over.
I'll shoot you an email.

KYLE: Just text me, dude.

TRAVIS: No can do. All plans go through the boss, so gotta use
the joint email. You know how it is, bro.

First of all, if she doesn't inspire rabid, unwarranted state pride and didn't write "Born to Run," she ain't the boss. Secondly, your balls belong in your pants or someone's mouth, not your woman's pocketbook. This is what relationships have become: Women bullying men into submission and men attending Jason Mraz concerts. It's like there are only two kinds of guys available these days: the crazed, insecure psycho who thinks being easily set off is manly and "old-fashioned," or the petrified, whipped ball-less guy who willingly walks on eggshells just to "keep the peace" with a wife or girlfriend. The whole relationship revolves around avoiding an ongoing argument that he has no clue what it's even about. But hey, as long as *she's* happy. He just runs around like a blank-staring disciple from the Captain Control Freak Congregation chanting, "Happy wife, happy life. She wears the pants . . . [*nervous laughter ensues*]." Yeah, she wears the pants, and you wear the high-waisted, ass-flattening mom jeans. What these guys should be saying is, "Happy wife, I have no life, I have no balls, and I cry during sex . . . when I finally get it once in a blue-balls moon." They should also be asking themselves what kind of a woman is attracted to a pandering pussy who agrees to a fancy Jack and Jill shower instead of a hilarious golden shower performed by little people at a Motel 6 bachelor party.

But this is the norm now. We all know this couple; the one depicted in network TV sitcoms (cut to hapless dad in an amorphic, button-down plaid shirt tightly tucked into wrinkle-resistant khakis being spoken to like a misbehaving eight-year-old by his domineering, no-nonsense wife who "just needs a day at the spa" because "she is the brains and the brawn behind this operation" per her testosterone-challenged husband). As she constantly criticizes and reprimands her husband, she looks like the bigger asshole for choosing somebody so inept.

While it's polite and considerate to let your spouse know your plans, it's pathetic to nervously ask permission. Can you imagine your grandfather asking grandma permission to grab a beer with the fellas? Nowadays, if a guy's buddy asks him to grab a beer, it's met with terror because his brain is scrambling to figure out how he's even going to broach the subject with his perpetually aggravated wife. By the look of panic on his face, you'd think somebody told him to run around Brazil yelling, "I Hate Soccer!"

Guys need a checklist to refer to when they're getting into that gray area of a relationship—the place where they straddle the line between still-a-man and the no-balls zone. So here's a list to help men reel it back in before it's too late.

GUYS, YOU MIGHT BE BALL-LESS IF:

• Your woman is going for Girls Night Out, and you're included.

• Your email address used to be 69isFine@yahoo.com, and now it includes an ampersand as in, Lindsey&EricLovebirds4ever@ soulmates.com.

• You now refer to pregnancy as a "Miracle!" and a "gift from God!" rather than a horrible reminder from that drunken night in Atlantic City with a Golden Nugget waitress named Crystal who looked like Jennifer Lopez when you went to bed with her but looked like George Lopez when you woke up with her.

• You don't watch much TV . . . unless there's a *Benson* rerun on because that family-friendly, clean humor is a hoot, and they don't make 'em like that anymore.

• When somebody says "Pandora," you name every charm on your wife's bracelet instead of making an inappropriate joke about the name of your friend D'Andre's baby.

• You need permission to tinkle (*Honey, do you mind if I go to the powder room?*), to get a haircut (*Honey, is it okay if I trim my bangs?*), and to die (*Honey, would it be a bother if I blow my brains out while you host your book club for the rest of the neighborhood Karens?*).

• You wear sandals/mandals, flip-flops, or Crocs, complete with the Disney collection of shoe charms.

• You think family-fun is the only kind of fun.

• Your idea of a good vacation involves a bubble bath complete with curling up with a cozy mystery and a scented candle while sipping a Frappuccino.

- You know what Frappuccino is.
- You take vacations to places that can only be referred to as quaint and charming.
- You carry around a Honey-Do list, and that list includes doing everything but your wife.
- You used to like to look at lesbian porn, now you look like a lesbian (the Vermont kind).
- You used to obsess about the three Bs: Booze, Boobs, and BJs. Now you obsess about the other triple Bs—Bed, Bath, and Beyond.
- The only digits that used to excite you were a girl's measurements and her phone number. The only digits that give you a rise now are improved cholesterol results and your ideal sleep number.

Fellas, just remember that when she finally pushes you over the edge, ask permission before you head to Wal-Mart to buy the duct tape, rope, shovel, tarps, and bleach.

DOUBLE DATES

I'm like a guy in relationships. I don't plan stuff with other couples, and if left alone, I eat Easy Cheese for dinner in my wife-beater. I'd rather give birth to an adult unicorn than partake in double dates and dinner parties. I love people, especially the ones I don't have to spend time with. They're so much more enjoyable that way. But it's really exhausting hanging with other couples pretending to care about "that pesky leak" they "couldn't find the source of for two months." *Oh no! Tell me more!* Or listening to their theories on why Donna—the divorcée next door—hasn't been seen in ten days. Maybe she doesn't want to go on a double date with you guys, so she has to hide all her new hookups from you. Blocking your texts and wearing a fake mustache to bring her groceries in wasn't enough of a hint that she hates your nosy guts?

I barely have enough energy to hang out with myself; now I have to sit with a couple of jabber jaws who have opinions on every single thing I don't give a shit about—from politics to health hacks (anything with the word *hack* in the title is automatically annoying). These long-winded wankers are like human Facebook posts.

The moment I'm invited on a double date, my panic attack starts. Most people are gross so I'm already convinced they're going to serve something with rogue cat litter and hair in it. But I try to remember relationships are all about sacrifices (at least that's what Pastor Cal tells all the couples on *Married at First Sight* who are paired with mental abusers) and I agree to take one for the team. When we arrived at their house, I knew it would stink worse than Yankee Candle at Christmas when we were told to remove our shoes. I should have followed the clues at the level of suckiness when I heard their names were Doug and Shelly. Who the fuck is named Doug or Shelly in 2021 outside of nursing homes or active retirement communities in Scottsdale, Arizona? To make matters worse, they're one of those "the glass is half full" kind of couples even after the wine glass was knocked over during a domestic dispute and permanently stained the carpet.

Right away, they start talking about their latest vacation. I caught my glazed-over reflection in the butter knife that I was contemplating plunging into my ears. My idea of a vacation is relaxing in the sun on a tropical beach or people-watching at the "happiest place on earth"—observing homicidal dads taking deep breaths before going postal on their families all while donning an *I'm so Goofy* t-shirt.

This couple starts talking about their vacation—and with people like this, it's never anywhere idyllic like Hawaii or Madrid. It's always somewhere war-torn, poverty-stricken, or a country ruled by a micropenis dictator. These weirdos are speaking as if they just returned from St. Tropez. "Yeah, we didn't want to do Guyana again because it wouldn't be fair to ignore all the other amazing places on this planet. So, this time we went to Nicaragua," says Shelly (with overly enunciated emphasis on the *-ragua* part). "Doug, I'm telling them about Ni-ca-ra-GUA. Is the foie gras ready?" Great, our meal rhymes with her story and is just as pretentious. At this point, all I could think of was diarrhea. I didn't feel it coming on or anything. I was just trying to fill my mind with more pleasant thoughts than vacationing in Zika's playground.

Shelly continues, "But when you go—and you HAVE TO go— you have to live as the natives do to truly experience the beauty of the country." I'm thinking, *where'd he find these fuckers?* Okay, so you want me to spend my entire vacation swatting flies and walking around shoeless begging for food while crying "mama, mama, mama" while playing with a three-legged feral dog? Where do I sign up! And no, Doug, I don't want to see your photos of the village scenery in all of its rotting wood and dust-choked-air glory. If I wanted to see something dusty and rotten, I'd have Charlie Rose open that robe of his. Do you think people who live in Venice say, "I'd love to visit Bridgeport, Connecticut and live as the natives do, and I hope I get shot and left in a burning building."?

The other problem is that when the two people who are already friends go out together, they have a system for splitting the bill. Now you add the outsiders, and you can kiss that convenience goodbye. There's always one prick at the table who wants to nickel and dime down to the number of wings each person had. And they always start with, "I don't mean to be petty but . . . ," which is really the bill-splitting version of "I don't mean to be racist but . . ."

And if you're the no-kid-couple joining the kid-couple, you may as well shoot yourself on the ride over. These people have nothing interesting to discuss unless you are on the edge of your seat hearing about what a little devil Timmy was when mommy put him to bed last night. *What? No way! Do you mean he didn't fall asleep right away and tried to get you to read another bedtime story? I've never heard of such a thing.* And hold the phone, everybody! They didn't just tell me that Maggie "wuvs her daddy this many," did they? *You've got to be shitting me! Kids never do this stuff.* How long am I supposed to act stunned? If you told me your kid could shapeshift into a giant everything bagel, or Gary Busey's teeth, you might have my attention and a second date.

Let's be honest, most couple's shit is annoying on its own. Now I have to double the annoyance factor by adding another couple into the mix? I'm not trying to get a job from these people; why do I have to be on my best behavior and wear give-a-shit makeup? Why am I the only one dreading sharing nicknamed appeteasers with people I'd otherwise avoid? I'm usually perturbed by at least three of them (one of which is me). The ideal situation is both you and your partner are so irritated by the other couple that you have something fun to talk about on the way home. "Can you believe Chris and Kelsey broke up for two weeks because he forgot to get her flowers for her 'workiversary'? And what the fuck is a Birkin bag? Is that where his balls and her personality have been hiding all night?" This is especially helpful for long-term relationships where you've run out of stuff to say to each other. Finding that couple to shit on is the glue that keeps you together.

The Hall Pass

I hate the hall pass. For those of you unfamiliar with it, it's when a couple "allows" each other a hall pass to have sex with their celebrity crush . . . as if that's ever going to happen. I'm pretty sure some balding, bloated middle school football coach isn't going to be the object of Charlize Theron's affection should she happen to be shooting a film in Ortonville, Minnesota. That's why couples are so agreeable to this—because they know there isn't a chance in hell of a hot celebrity wanting to bang their spouse. They're a dumpy Merrells-wearing dud with zero options, and even *they* don't want to bang their spouse.

All I know is that if I crossed paths with one of my celebrity crushes like Mike Ness or Robert Downey Jr., and I was feeling lucky (i.e., chloroform rags locked and loaded in my purse), I wouldn't ask anyone's permission, including my hall pass. You might call it sexual harassment, but I just call it old-fashioned preparedness.

"YOU Should Love Me No Matter What"

Unconditional love is for people without options. I'm pretty sure I shouldn't love you if I find out you tickle toddlers' ballsacks, kick kittens, curb-stomp old people, or have a bedside pee bottle.

But in most cases, "You should love me no matter what" is a demand exclaimed by a person in a romantic relationship who is suddenly gross. What constitutes gross is subjective to the partner of said gross person. Perhaps you're married to a fella who swept you off your feet with his kind heart, sense of humor, healthy life-style, and impressive cooking skills. Fast forward five years, and he looks like he ate himself—twice. Now his cooking skills consist of heating up a Whopper in the microwave. But he's still a gosh darn riot, especially when he has to wipe his ass with a rag attached to a broom handle. He used to be a stallion in bed, but now he's more like a pregnant two-toed sloth. Sure, you love the son of a gun because he's still the same person inside—even though the person you're looking for is buried deeper than an underground presiden-tial bunker beneath a hill of lipomas. When people say, "You should love me no matter what," what they really mean is, "You should be attracted to me no matter what." They can be utterly neglectful of themselves and diminish all efforts to keep the spark of attraction alive, yet they act stunned when your desire diminishes along with their lack of effort. "Honey, can you vacuum the cat litter out of my gunt? I can't reach."

It's not always a weight thing that turns people off. It could be slacking on oral hygiene or calling their alcoholism *unwinding* or *family tradition.* Or, maybe a woman had long, silky blonde hair when she met her boyfriend. But since they've been together for a while, she let it go back to mousy brown and cropped it into what she deems a "sassy" style. What it looks like to the rest of the world is that white trash mom-haircut done in the kitchen "salon" of a trailer parked in the middle of the woods in bum-fuck Kentucky. While some guys might not care, other guys' dicks shrivel up like the six-week-old grapes you forgot about in the back of the fridge. Of course, she can grow her hair back, but she knows her boyfriend's turned off. She decides to keep the rat's nest, insisting he should love her no matter what. In his most loving voice, he informs her he does love her. That love is why he's not telling her he's getting blow jobs from a prostitute whose head doesn't look like a Bichon Frise when he glances down at it.

PaRt 2

TRiGGa' PLeaSE

8

UpTight_y Whi_ey

The Uptighty Whitey is an increasingly popular breed of white people. It is most often found in its natural habitat of corner offices, suburbia, and wellness retreats. The Uptighty Whitey presumptuously fancies themself the representative for all whites, as well as the unsolicited spokesperson for most minorities. The Uptighty Whitey also arrogantly believes they embody what all minorities want from *woke* whites.

There was a time when being an *uptight white* meant something completely different than the douchebags we're now accustomed to. There was a time when any white person was considered uptight simply due to their love of turtlenecks, refusal to associate with non-whites, and lack of zest when it comes to pretty much anything. But times have changed, and so has whitey's political landscape—the one landscape they can't pay Mexicans to maintain.

You can spot an Uptighty Whitey by some telltale features, such as creating extra-long words or phrases to avoid offending various groups, including those less white or less outfitted in North Face attire than they are. Another telltale feature is words that don't match their actions, such as verbally championing the plight of blacks or Hispanics yet frantically rolling up their windows and locking their doors when encountering said compadres at a traffic light.

Identifying an Uptighty Whitey can be tricky as they come in many varieties. Beginners can identify the more overt ones by their hippy therapist style. It includes sandals all year long, glasses to accentuate pondering facial expressions, and a whispery speaking-style suggesting they're never ruffled—even though they're secretly a simmering pot of buried rage (*Stop talking in your ASMR serial killer voice; it's giving me nightmares!*). They have an affinity for anything khaki-colored, including cargo shorts, sofas, and shade of teeth. This uptight white is often found at protests, Starbucks, community theaters, private ivy-covered college campuses, and indoor rock-climbing facilities.

You can also spot them at comedy shows. Their eyes dart around for the exit when the comic begins talking about the difference between blacks and whites.

"Whites have no rhythm, but blacks even *pray* with rhythm."

At this point, they are standing up.

"Whites talk like nerds, but blacks sound cool even using *made-up* words."

At this point, they are stepping on people's toes and knocking over drinks off other people's tables– "*'scuse me . . . 'scuse me ...*", and he is . . . outta there.

Whitey will make it to the bathroom as they dry heave with disgust over the perpetuation of "racism" disguised as humor. They return to their seat at the end of the white comic's set, just as a black comic comes to the stage. Before the comic even opens their mouth, the Uptighty Whitey is clapping like an overzealous seal while grinning—as if Megan Fox is blowing him under the table. He's confident this new comic is going to be fucking awesome. When the comic talks about the differences between blacks and whites, the Uptighty Whitey is slapping his knee like he's swatting gnats during one of his super white nature hikes as he frantically nods his head in unbridled agreement.

A version that's a bit more difficult to identify is the one found in your everyday settings. At first glance, you might think the male

is an insurance executive or a professional golfer with his classi-
cally safe Peter Gun haircut, Sperry docksiders (never worn on
work days; reserved only for loose occasions such as guy's night
at PF Chang's), and his Volvo keychain strategically placed on the
table to flaunt that he's financially superior, yet sensible with his
transportation decisions. His non-ethnic/non-exotic wife goes
unnoticed in most crowds with her puffy blonde bob, her smart
Talbot's slacks (if they're from Talbot's, they're slacks, not pants),
and a nautical summer scarf that shows her pizazz and sense of
adventure. This well-to-do twosome enjoys criticizing others for
being unevolved and unsympathetic to the struggles of those they
deem less fortunate. They're very good at voicing their concerns
and scolding fellow whites for "not making a difference," yet there's
no physical evidence of them practicing what they preach.

It's pretty exciting to observe an uptight white in different
social settings. It's an excellent opportunity to showcase their keen
memorization of buzzwords and phrases disguised as knowledge
and understanding of all people. If you're lucky enough to attend
a graduation party or bridal shower for an uptight white, you can
catch bits and pieces of conversations around the room that might
include, "... and I said to Bob, 'Black lives matter. We must let *those
people* know we agree.'" Meanwhile, there isn't one black person at
the party. No one even has a tan. The only hint of color is Maura
O'Leary's sunburn because she forgot to wear sunblock to the
twins' soccer game (and because she's a fair-skinned boozer whose
facial blood vessels look like they've been in a pot of boiling cabbage
all day).

If you happen to encounter the aforementioned white, do not
make the mistake of engaging in any conversation, not even generic
topics like the weather. Uptighty Whitey will use that as a chance

to crowbar in examples of his sensitivity to the suffering and simultaneously shame you for being so blasé.

"Beautiful day, isn't it, Phil?"

"Beautiful to who? Not to the Syrian refugees who don't know where they're going to sleep tonight." (Meanwhile, they're not sleeping at Phil's despite his deep concern and worry)

Another snafu you might run into is challenging the politically correct rhetoric of this non-practicing "lover of all men." If you ask Whitey how many minorities live in his neighborhood, you'll never get an actual answer. But you *will* learn that he has "many black friends" and he works "with several Hispanics." If you press for names, he will only provide you with the extension for housekeeping at his office.

The best way to avoid engaging with this monster of politically correct verbal diarrhea is to simply ask, "¿Se habla Español?" He'll suddenly remember that he has to make an important phone call as he pats his back pocket to ensure his wallet is still there.

9

ANGRY "PaTRioTic" GUy

Angry "Patriotic" Guy (APG) is a walking jambalaya of contradictions, a riddle within a riddle. He ties most of his stances into what he deems it is to be a "real" man. And according to APG's regular demeanor, being a real man is an awareness that somebody is always out to get him. Whether it be the fast-food worker who forgot to hold the lettuce, the dude who accidentally brushed against him at the bar, or the government using expensive satellites and vaccines just to spy on him rounding third base with cousin Tammi out behind the woodshed, APG is always prepared to teach a lesson because he "DESERVES RESPECT!" He mistakes people trying to avoid a run-in with a crazed animal as being respected. Poor dummy.

APG isn't to be confused with RPG (Real Patriotic Guy). RPG is a respectful and respectable guy who minds his own business, treats people kindly, and isn't easily triggered like Bill O'Reilly at an airport. APG is most often found in his native environment of subservient women's vaginas; GNC; driving eighty miles per hour in a breakdown lane—because "only pussies wait their turn in traffic and consider the safety of others!"—and on Facebook perusing critical "news" stories from petulant political memes and copied/pasted posts created by some emotionally deficient whitey from a city that's famous for community events that end in *fest* (Pumpkinfest, Wild Westfest, Dipshitfest).

He's a fella who's proficient in mumbo-jumbo and conflicting stances. He mocks others for their lack of bravery and claims he fears nothing. Yet, he's armed to the teeth because apparently, he fears "they" are going to take away his rights any day now ("any day now" has been his entire adult life, according to his perpetual panic-rantings). He claims to be a responsible gun owner but acts like an unhinged lunatic towards anyone who doesn't want unhinged lunatics to own guns. You can be pro-gun, but if you think certain precautions should be in place, his brain will explode like a Devastator bullet in a tin can. In a crazed fashion, APG will furiously chant "second amendment!" without a full knowledge of its origins. The idea that the world has changed since a document from the 1700s was written is irrelevant to this surface-only thinker. He can't comprehend that it wasn't put in place for every paranoid jerkoff who grills hot dogs in their driveway next to a dilapidated speedboat on their lawn. They'll also suggest that teachers should have to carry guns in case there's a school shooter on the loose. Most of these teachers couldn't even curb the bullying that turned the kid into a mass murderer in the first place. You think some guy in corduroy chinos and an argyle vest is miraculously going to turn into John Wick?

Any debate that requires facts, data, or extrapolatory information is answered with memorized (although misquoted and misinterpreted) lines from the US Constitution or Bible and an "interesting nugget" from a podcast, followed by the quippy comment, "just think about it." He may even use the statement "all lives matter," with the caveat that those lives aren't of a different skin tone, sexual orientation, political view, income bracket, or region of the country from him. He often lets you know how much he "LOVES JESUS!" and his "GODDAMN COUNTRY!" but always seems riled up and hypertensive when letting you know. He fiercely supports rights and freedom . . . unless they're others' freedoms that have zero impact on him whatsoever. The idea that a football player could take a knee during the national anthem is only one of many things APG takes personal offense to and can't examine beyond a surface level. "How dare you disrespect the 'mercan flag! (not to be confused with a merkin flag which is a patriotic pubic wig). "Men fought for your right to . . ." He doesn't seem to fathom that his argument only further backs up the kneeler, not him.

APG is proud of something he didn't achieve. He's proud of happenstance. He was born in America. *Freedom, freedom, freedom.* Yet, as he's trying to read this—before sharing it on the dark web to add his own smoky flavor of hate-smeared mockery—he's near stroke-level cursing me out as a "TRAITOR!!!" rather than praising me for exercising my American right to freedom of speech that he supposedly finds so precious. He'll support freedom of speech for nonsensical conspiracy theories that resemble a script for a hilarious mockumentary starring Eugene Levy but rage over anything requiring deeper comprehension.

Although his identity revolves around his "devotion" to his country, he couldn't give a shit about anyone else living in it if they're not identical to him. While the military/real patriots (who he vehemently claims to support) sacrifice their lives for the rest of us, APG finds it far too much of a sacrifice to slap a mask on for twenty minutes while he's in public. He prefers to bully and terrorize innocent workers—who are risking their lives for adult babies like him—rather than just get in, grab his cigs and Flamin' Hot Cheetos, get out, and take his mask off in his American flag-flying pickup truck. He's a laissez-faire kind of a guy when it comes to pandemics and the safety of others. "I WILL NOT WEAR A FACE DIAPER! I ain't a pussy! I ain't wearin' no mask and looking like I'm afraid of anything!" But he's afraid of looking afraid? Or is he afraid of looking like a pussy? Or is it both? Doesn't that make him a bigger pussy?

Doesn't his fear of appearing fearful actually make him *more* fearful? Do they not make fryolator-scented masks with American Eagles on them?

APG reminds everyone via barstool ramblings, bumper stickers, and online posts that he bleeds red, white, and blue—mostly from his rectum because this tightly-wound, argumentative human bullhorn is loaded with hemorrhoids and hardened stool. Maybe he'd be less angry if he could poop adequately.

If you're not sure whether you're in the presence of an APG, always proceed with caution. He comes in the well-to-do, privileged variety too. But remember, you can buy an education. You can buy an American flag muscle shirt. But you can't pick your friend's nose, even if it's not covered by a mask. I think that's the point, right?

10

The Wokey Pokey

♫ *You put your right finger in, you take your right finger out,*
  you put your right finger in, and you wag it all about.
  You do the Wokey Pokey and yell at everyone.
  You hate to ever have fun. ♪

Remember the good old days when being politically correct (PC) was a mere annoyance that only involved a couple of hours of goofing off at work (better known as sensitivity training) and memorizing a few wordy terms to replace offensive ones assholes continued using in private anyhow (and in Philly . . . and in frat houses . . . and at St. Patrick's Day parades)? There were literally three things we had to remember. Handicap rolled on over to disabled, fat lumbered its way over to weight-challenged, and black was no longer acceptable even to describe tarry stool (so long early colon cancer detection).

When did we become a society of joyless, clueless, hyper-alert, overly sensitive, humorless windbags who are easily offended by everything? We contend with completely manufactured issues that are supposed to bring us together but succeed only in dividing us further. And to be clear, this no longer applies exclusively to PC proponents. The America-obsessed, possessed "patriots" are cut from the same cloth. They get infuriated over people who want to use PC terminology, yet they flip their ugly-flat-wide-brim-hat-wearing-lids-with-sunglasses-on-top if you don't want to use their outdated, booze-infused favorites.

The news is full of unsuspecting people being demonized for having the nerve to use a once non-threatening word or phrase that they had no clue was now a red flag for latent evil. There was even a teacher blasted for asking her students to sit Indian-style for an exercise.

And God forbid you have the gall to feel uncomfortable when you encounter a laser-focused middle-eastern fella in a suspiciously crisp *God Bless America* t-shirt with a rice cooker in his *I Love NY* backpack hopping on the subway. You'll be exposed as a paranoid, profiling racist. Then he sues you and uses his winnings to pay for flight school and a truck full of burner phones and radio controllers, but somehow, you're the jerk-face. "See something, say something"? More like, "See something? How dare you! Only racists see suspicious activity."

On the one hand, we're being scolded for using so-called nasty words, but then we're being called equally nasty names in return. Has *Indian* always been an insult, or did some annoying white nincompoop with an agenda and a Prius decide to make it one? If *sitting Indian style* is offensive, it's only a matter of time before *eating family-style* is off the table. Uh oh, some wimp's feelings might get hurt because he doesn't have a two-parent family. Better sue Olive Garden for discriminatory marketing. At a minimum, they should be sued for calling their food Italian. Now *that's* offensive.

I have a friend who was fired from her job because she couldn't understand a person's accent on the phone. She wasn't rude or inappropriate about it; she simply requested clarification because she couldn't understand what the person said. Hell, I can't even understand most fellow Americans, so I think it's reasonable that a foreign accent might be difficult for some to decipher.

I wish society would stop inciting people to be upset about everything, especially things without ill-intent or malice. A woman on Twitter called me uptight for writing a satirical article for *Madhouse Magazine* about Cardi B selling ice cream bars called WAP (Wet-Ass Pussicles) shaped like her vagina. I'm guessing she believes "female empowerment" involves keeping nothing private, including your privates and their level of delectability. But wasn't *she* the uptight one for taking offense to something so goofy? We'd probably be a much happier country if people didn't manufacture all this divisiveness by taking harmless things and making them poisonous—especially things that don't have origins in hatred or bigotry. In fact, I think people's well-intentioned yet way too aggressive messaging is what's emboldening the bigots and bullies.

I can't remember what is and isn't on the list of acceptable terminology today but most of us, myself included, have adjusted and accepted the changes. For instance, you can't say *hungry*. You have to say *food insecure*. You can't say *gay*, you have to say *meteorologist*. And you can't say *pussy* anymore; you have to say *in their twenties.* I don't need some hypervigilant, phony, do-gooder interpreting the meaning of my words to fit their agenda just as I don't need some aggressively proud-for-no-good-reason weirdo trying to convince everybody that being able to say the "n" word, or calling somebody a "fag" is imperative to their rights and freedoms (insert head-smack here).

We're making innocuous names offensive and putting everybody in a state of perpetual PMS. Is it getting to the point where we're going to have to change classic song titles too? "Stairway to Heaven" is going to become "Handicap Accessible Ramp to Your Idea of Utopia." Fleetwood Mac's hit, "Gypsy," will now be known as

"Free-spirited Romani Person Who Doesn't Rob People Despite No Known Legitimate Source of Income." And "You've Lost that Lovin' Feelin'" will be renamed, "Don't Worry. It Happens to Every Guy. There's Medication for It."

Suddenly, everyone is a deputy in the PC police. They claim to denounce using labels, but if something doesn't fit their narrative, the labels are unleashed like a fart in a Fiat after a late-night trip to Taco Bell. I wish I could put into words what I think of them, but I don't believe they've come up with a PC term for pretentious blow-hard ass-clown yet.

11

If YOU WaNT My BOdy

aND YOU ThiNK I'm SeXy,

It's PRobablY SeXUAL HaRASSmenT

Your supervisor asks you to meet at his place for a dinner meeting to discuss a promotion. Is this: **A.** *Quid pro quo* **B.** *A hostile work environment* **C.** *1982*

That's a question from the sexual harassment training quiz my friend had to take at his new job. Of course, answer C wasn't an option but come on. Really? Isn't it safe to say that every scenario presented in these trainings is a no-no? These days, you can't even sniff your secretary's chair without it being considered sexual harassment.

I'm all for treating people fairly and properly, but we need to calm down on what we consider inappropriate, actionable, or hostile for chrissakes. Take, for example, Shakira's hips. Everyone knows those suckers don't lie. My cousin's in the breakroom at work when highlights from the Super Bowl halftime show pop on. His buddy says, "Dude, she's so hot." Next thing you know, he's fired for his "offensive" remarks because another employee walked in, heard the comment, and ran to HR to tattle on him. What harm was done? It wasn't directed at her, or maybe that's what pissed her off. Why should that guy be punished because of some whiner's self-esteem issues? If I walked in on that comment, I'd pull up a chair and chime in. And for the record, my hips don't lie, my lips don't tattle, but my bra's told a few fibs over the years. I think it's more despicable to get somebody fired for an innocuous comment than it is to say "titties" at work. The problem with accommodating complaints like this is that we never consider how hostile the drama is. Or how traumatizing it is to have to coddle people who wear friendship beads.

Of course, I disapprove of sexual harassment. I've been subjected to it many times. Heck, I even perpetrated it regularly at one job. When you control the PA system at a company full of men, it would be a crime not to use it for inappropriate announcements like, "Dave, Mark from Audio Maxipad is on line one. Speaking of maxipads, your wife also called and asked if you could pick some up on the way home."

But I never got in trouble for it. Do you know why? Because it was silly, and healthy people like to laugh, not create overblown tension and turn everything into a learning moment.

Nobody should be put in an uncomfortable sexual position at work—especially sixty-nine (unless you have a sturdy conference table)—just as nobody should fear for their job if they refuse to do certain things. But let's stop being dramatic and ridiculous by pretending every little thing is an encroachment. Of course, there are Louis CKs doing things to make you feel weird, intimidated, and violated. Those people should be reported and dealt with accordingly. But if you report a guy who says your hair looks nice, maybe it should be fair game to report your over-the-top hysterical reaction that also creates an uncomfortable work environment. To me, walking on eggshells every time I'm in the company of another person seems a lot more trauma-inducing than knowing Larry from IT thinks I look nice today. If you don't like it, say so. If they ignore your request to stop, you can either report it, or you can secretly subscribe them to a Filipino dating site via their work computer and "accidentally" leave the screen on with the images of "twenty-year-old women" who look twelve . . . or call their wife pretending to be his knocked-up mistress . . . or sprinkle MiraLAX in their coffee and watch some real shit get started . . . literally.

You can't even flirt anymore without being villainized. Isn't this why married people work outside of the home? And why isn't it sexual harassment when a chick is giving guys boners all day long? My friend used to work for a woman who had giant melon boobs. She wore tight, see-through tops without a bra. If he wanted to know the outside temperature, he just looked at her sundials. Sure it was uncomfortable and awkward, but he took it like a grown-up. He didn't cry and complain. He masturbated in the men's bathroom stall during breaks because he was a gentleman.

And why is it considered "a hoot" when the office gals objectify men? Who wants to listen to a bunch of cackling hens returning from Applebee's talking about the waiter's "perfect buns" and how well he "takes orders"? Should we run to HR every time one of these lame innuendos or puns is used in the workplace?

POP QUIZ:

My coworker posted a picture on Facebook of me in my bathing suit from the company picnic. Now they're making fun of me. Is this:

    A. Sexual harassment

    B. A hostile work environment

    C. Warranted. Sideburns are for men's faces, not ladies' groins

Is it sexual harassment if a coworker asks to turn up the boob tube in the breakroom?

    A. Only if he makes a dial-turning gesture with his fingers

B. Who the hell says boob tube? How is a 90-year-old
    still working?

C. Tee hee! He said "boob"

Anyone born after 1991 considers themselves a victim of sexual harassment. I'm pretty sure they fly out of the womb with a lawyer and paperwork accusing the doctor of inappropriate touching. Here's the bottom line: if a coworker says your dress is pretty, say "thank you." If your coworker creeps up behind you, rubs your shoulders, and whispers in your ear "your dress is pretty" with his dick in your back, give Gloria Allred a ring. Or head to the nearest La Quinta motel. I'm not here to judge.

12

FaItiTUdE

When I used to work with the public, people thought nothing of saying things to me like, "Oh my God, there's nothing to you. I bet you don't even eat!" "If you turn sideways, you'll disappear." "Wow, you are so skinny; you must be anorexic." I wanted to say, "Wow, you're so rude. You must be . . . a cunt!" Maybe it's because I could always hold (and rub) my own, but the Body Shamers Police never showed up to protect my psyche. Nobody was triggered by the slew of insults hurled at me. But would these people ever go up to a fat person and be like, "Holy shit, you're HUGE! You must have sleep apnea—and really chafed inner thighs"? Of course, they wouldn't because that's cruel and politically incorrect. But somehow, berating a stranger for not having a Carnival-cruise-ship-all-inclusive-buffet-body is okay.

Society now uses the mantra *Good for her* as a warrior call for female empowerment and solidarity. The term is popular amongst Oprah disciples, ranch dressing users, Adirondack chair lovers, and people who don't know what's happening but love to use catchphrases.

My first exposure to this was when I was at lunch with a friend, Candy. We were seated by the window when a woman walked by with some coworkers. Candy began to make a comment along the lines of "what was she thinking," but she quickly changed her tune and said, "You know what, good for her." The woman was wearing a suit-jacket and miniskirt that wouldn't have been mini had she purchased it in the correct size (one acre). The outfit was complete with pleather fold-over ankle boots that were totally cool . . . if she were a self-proclaimed sexually ambiguous male lead singer of an eighties British pop group. Oh, and did I mention her legs looked like two bags of cement that somebody tiptoed on when they were wet? What I'm trying to say is, the appropriate response was, "What in tarnation was this silly man of a gal thinking?"—unless you live in Alabama; then the appropriate response would've been, "Now that's a classy lady, right there."

So, I said to Candy, "Why 'good for her'?" Candy said, "I love empowered women. I think it's great that she's comfortable with her body and doesn't care what other people think. Good for her! Who are we to judge?" However, about fifteen minutes before this, Candy was judging—with much disgust—a beautiful, well-endowed mutual friend for wearing cleavage-exposing tops. Her tit-rage was so over the top and scary it's as if she suddenly turned into Mel Gibson and the tits were two big jiggly Jews. It seems to me that the female solidarity rules aren't consistent.

I'm not saying people should be made fun of or treated poorly. I'm saying that it's hypocritical to be vindictive towards people of below-average size yet protective of those of above-average size. Obesity and anorexia are both eating disorders, but obese people are coddled, glorified, and sympathized with, while anorexic individuals are treated as though they're just vain. Why do average-sized or thin people have to sit back and take it when bombarded with insults for *not* being fat, but an activist group is formed whenever there's a supposed fat-shamer on the loose?

Going through life as a scrawny female with fun bags that are more like tea bags hasn't been a picnic, but I certainly don't expect special treatment because of it. Do you know how humiliating it is to look like an X-ray in a tube top with arms that look like brown angora-coated toothpicks when you go to the beach? But nobody worried about my feelings when pointing out all these flaws to me.

"Oh my God, thank you for telling me! I had no idea my Feed-The-Children-esque upper body wasn't a turn on." Thank God for honest strangers; otherwise, I'd be walking around with a sassy look on my face and my hand on my protruding hipbone, declaring, "I'm fine yo! Haters be frontin'" just like my plus-size counterparts do when obnoxiously bragging about their physiques. How confident can a person truly be if they feel they have to ram it down your throat the way they ram Jimmy Dean's pancakes-on-a-stick down their throats?

How about being humble regardless of your size and not criticizing people who happen to have the opposite weight problem or body type if you're unwilling to take criticism about your own? And how come you never see guys like Billy Gardell or Fat Joe posting naked pictures with daffodils coming out of their asses with #juicy and #lovemycurves to punctuate their confidence? I guarantee they'd be laughed at and considered the butt of the joke (pun intended) by the same asshats who demand everyone praise females who post similar images.

It's getting old hearing large women brag about how fantastic their bodies are and that they're "real." Would it be acceptable if I said, "*Real* women don't have to stand over a mirror to see their hoo-has"? Or, how about, "Real women don't grunt when pooping"? How about saying, "Real women come in all shapes and sizes, and nobody is better than anybody else because of their ability to lose a pair of panties in their ass." I'm so sick of the rhetoric: "Real women have curves. Men want something they can grab onto." Um, isn't that what my throat is for?

13

GeNdER ExTeNdER

While it may seem exhausting to keep up with all the gender and sexuality terminology, I'm not upset about it like some paranoid pantywaist who transfers their kids to a private school just to avoid the "danger" of calling somebody *they* instead of *she*. Newsflash: If your kid has gender identity issues, trapping them in an environment full of entitled fucktards isn't going to change anything. And ask yourself why you think gaining knowledge about things you're unfamiliar with is indoctrination, but having a group of people wearing identical attire with identical thoughts isn't. And while it is comical to watch people overreact to stuff they can't comprehend; it's getting harder to keep up with all these identifiers and what they mean.

I'm concerned I'm going to offend somebody because I don't know what's what. You have: Binary, non-binary, gender-neutral (even goes with plaid!), genderfluid (sounds messy; do I need a pantyliner?), agender, bigender (not to be confused with "Bye gender, don't need *you* anymore"), genderqueer, trigender (but please don't fail gender), intergender, gender-questioning (just don't answer without a lawyer present), gender-variant, gender-more, genderless, gender-sometimes (but not tonight honey; I have a headache), cisgender, swing and a misgender, chicken genders, pots and pangender, transgender, can-but-won't gender, and last but not least, Caitlyn-gender.

Individuals are even taking this beyond gender, claiming to be varied species or objects on different days. When someone says, "Today, I identify as a dolphin," I say, "Every day, I identify you as an asshole." If you're going to identify as a different species, the only one that makes sense is a silly goose because now you're just being dopey. Going from LGBT to LGBTQ to LGBTQIAKLMNOP has made me go from OK to WTF to TMI! The K stands for kink. I understand gender identifiers, but why do strangers need to know your sexual proclivities? Put that on a dating app, not on your car windows. When will they add FF for foot fetish, CM for chronic masturbator, and SC for serial cheater? Eventually, they're going to have to decide if GB is still for gay and bisexual or for the people who like to dress like giant babies. (Don't you want to change that diaper?)

I understand being born in the wrong body because I was born in the wrong body with the wrong nationality. I'm Italian, yet I don't identify with being a loud-mouthed, gold-jewelry-wearing, proud-for-no-reason cafone who shows they have no class by constantly calling things classy (this example only applies to American Italians of a certain unnamed region). In my mind, I'm a leggy, Swedish, natural stunner trapped in a short, hairy, sallow-skinned body. But I can't get upset when strangers don't pick up on that just by looking at me, especially when my body suggests I'm a very haggard, frizzy-haired, poor man's miniature Susanna Hoffs. (I'll even walk like an Egyptian after too much rum cake and a Benadryl).

People need to accept that sometimes a person is born in the wrong body. They should also put themselves in the other person's men-sized-thirteen stilettos and understand the pain, fear, confusion, and trauma they have endured. We know that a man's mind and soul can be in a woman's body and vice-versa. There are hormones and surgery to help them achieve their true identity. However, a person cannot be a lamp, a cheetah, or a Jacobean lily, no matter how much they insist they were born as one. The point is that if you're a kind person, that's what I'm going to judge you on. I don't judge on sexual identity or sexual preference. As long as you're not one of those goddamn Jehovah's Witnesses, you're A-OKAY in my book.*

*If you had no idea that was a joke,
 please stop reading this book

14

Patty PaRty PoopeR

Patty Party Pooper (Triple P) is an irascible, politically-charged off-shoot of the better-known, socially lethargic Debbie Downer. With her undetectable charm, perpetually wagging finger, and her female empowerment mumbo jumbo, it's impossible to mistake Triple P for someone enjoyable.

In the past, many partygoers would roll their eyes in disappoint-ment if they got stuck in an awkward conversation with Debbie Downer. She wasn't annoying because she was pushy or opinion-ated; she was annoying because she was mopey and dull. Why is her cat always missing and her colon always misfiring? Maybe the cat keeps running away because he's had enough of her irritable bowel mishaps.

However, in recent years, many party guests are now hungering for the depressive bewitchery of Debbie Downer to blunt the Taser-like side-effects of an involuntary debate with Triple P. It's easy to identify one of these nettlesome creatures by some stock features.

- As insufferable as Marjorie Taylor Greene
- Jaw always going like a yippy chihuahua
- Pointing finger always locked and loaded
- Go-to karaoke song is "Fight Song" by Rachel Platten
- Devoid of any humor
- Waits for others to joke around so she can lambaste them or their ignorant insensitivity
- Wants to be loved for who she is, not how she looks (but that's only because the latter is not an option)

- Claims to be feminist but accuses any successful, beautiful woman of sleeping her way to the top
- Regularly mentions her alma mater and the foreign countries she's concerned about

She insists that the only reason she's single is that men are intimidated by her strength and intelligence. Maybe "strength" is code for "annoying personality," and "intelligence" is code for "not hot enough to tolerate the annoying personality." But even armed with these identifying traits, it's almost impossible to avoid a Triple P.

Recently I was at a sixtieth-anniversary party. My main concern wasn't making friends and debating politics. I was making sure the Metamucil-crusted baked scrod and tapioca pudding I ate didn't hit me like a torpedo blasting through a Krazy Straw. While I was quietly doing preemptive Kegel exercises tableside, I was also participating in the inane chitchat. The couple next to me mentioned that their son was starting third grade when Triple P piped in with, "Speaking of third grade, how about the kids being separated from their parents at the border?" Perfect conversation for a festive celebration of two people too stubborn to divorce and too lazy to pull the plug . . . on the other's oxygen tank.

But it was on. Triple P aggressively stood up yet still appeared to be seated, considering she was the size of a garden gnome. (Side note: Ever notice, the smaller the stature, the bigger the mouth?) She said, "I don't mean to be a Debbie Downer, but I don't know how anyone could say they don't have an opinion on the wall."

And I don't know how anyone could say to Triple P, "Would you like to come to my party?" How dare she call herself a Debbie

Downer. I would've paid for one of Deb's loose-stool sagas at that point just to avoid the inevitable divisive yammering that was headed our way.

For somebody with T-Rex proportions, I was amazed at how well she repeatedly patted herself on the back for being the hero in story after story of injustice. I realized that the other guests were only appeasing her in an attempt to shut her up after hearing the umpteenth tale in which she was either victim, hero, or both. But how could all these *What Would You Do?* moments happen without John Quiñones?

I felt like *I* was on *What Would You Do?* and needed an escape plan by this time. But if you can't escape and must engage, be warned: for anyone foolish enough to participate in Triple P's espousing about social issues, there is no correct response. If you agree with her, she feels vindicated and thus gets louder. If you disagree with her, she feels attacked and thus gets louder. If you slit your wrists and jam knives into your ears, she reaches into her well of Oprah-isms and encourages you to live . . . not for yourself, but so she'll have another heroic story to tell at the next party.

Don't be fooled, though; not all Triple Ps are social justice mouthpieces. The equally horrible Triple P's are the weirdos who try to crowbar their beliefs (and non-beliefs of real things) into every conversation. I was talking about vintage Yankees—specifically, Dave Winfield—when some dude I didn't know came over using the segue, "He must be like a hundred now. Wonder if *he's* whining about reparations." He then did a creepy laugh and that thing people do with their elbow to suggest we were in on some joke together. I knew not to bite, but the guy I was talking to got sucked in, and next thing I know, I'm listening to a grown man who thinks

Satan-worshipping, baby-eating pedophiles are real, but Sandy Hook isn't. Did this fucker eat the potato salad that was sitting in the sun for four hours? Was it his parents or his schoolmates who rejected him all his life? Or both? Like, how is this creature even formed? He's a little easier to escape from than social-justice-fueled Triple P, though. Just tell him you have to excuse yourself because you have the runs from the spicy Mexican baby you ate earlier.

BUNS N' POSES

Growing up in an image-conscious Italian family, I was taught that a presentable appearance was a sign of self-respect and respect for others. Back in the pre-proud-of-yourself-for-no-reason era, people would feel shame and embarrassment if seen in anything but their best. But do you see the way people leave the house nowadays: disheveled hair, fur-coated stretch pants, and rubber slippers with half of the soles chewed off by a pet ferret. They look like they just escaped a house fire and somehow ended up at Walmart in a diet soda coma.

Political correctness has put the kibosh on vanity sanity and everything we once knew about functioning in society. The saying *dress for the job you want, not the job you have* has turned into, *dress like you lost your job—and your mind—and you're going to go back and car-bomb the guy who fired you.* And forget about *dress to impress.* Now it's *dress like you couldn't care less. And if it doesn't fit, go ahead, show 'em your shit. Oh, and if your toenails look like melted candles, go ahead, show them off in sandals!* Because what do people say? "As long as I'm comfortable," in that punchable smug tone. As long as I'm comfortable? Really? Are tits tucked into sweatpants more comfortable than a bra? I suppose that's a question only a comic book shop owner can answer.

Having no shame seems to be the new badge of honor representing the "I don't care what other people think!" mentality. There's a difference between admitting you love the Charlotte Hornets and not caring what other people think versus walking around with an ass-vacuum that's sucking in most of your shorts and not caring what other people think. But people have no shame anymore, not even in front of their kids. If you want to teach your kids about the birds and the bees (and the STDs), take them to the Seaside Heights Jersey Shore boardwalk. Maybe I'm getting too uptight, but the bathing suits seem to have less material than a white bearded comedian telling pot jokes. I saw one parent strutting around with giant bologna tits in a tiny G-string, doing downward dog to get stuff out of the cooler. I said to my friend, "Do you believe this? That thong doesn't even cover . . . his ball sack." You could see everything: the bat, the balls, and the dugout.

We live in such a politically correct culture that everything that should be incorrect is correct, and everything abnormal is normal. And you know why that is? It's because we're afraid to hurt people's feelings. Newsflash: we may not be hurting people's feelings, but I'm definitely hurting my tongue every time I have to bite it when I see a guy with double-D titties in a retro Ric Flair tank top. When I see a grown man's exposed ass crack in his Dorito-stained Yosemite Sam pajama bottoms, I don't think, "Good for him! As long as he's comfortable!" I think, "What's going to happen when his mother dies, and he can't live in the basement anymore?"

People are such babies they can't even handle the idea that maybe a halter top isn't a good idea if it's not strong enough to halt what's in it. We have to tell everybody how great they are so they can walk around like conceited, human Hot Pockets pointing to body parts I don't want to be familiar with while making the "Mm-hmm" face. Instead of a little bit of gentle honesty, we go to the other extreme and say, "If you're five feet tall, and five feet wide with C-section scars, stretch marks, a tramp stamp, and a belly ring that looks like a superintendent's keychain, you should definitely wear a belly shirt that makes your stomach look like a tube sock filled with quarters. And please, match it up with a pair of two-sizes-too-small, out-of-season white pants that outline your camel toe like the Big Dipper in a laser light show."

The worst is the short-shorts epidemic because teens and kids are wearing them. If I can determine what stage of puberty someone's in based on the labia air vents in their Hollister cutoffs, they have some seriously wimpy parents. They don't want to hurt their kids' feelings and tell them *no* because "it might damage their self-esteem." Parents are now equating boundaries such as "don't wear pants that start below your hemorrhoids" with punching your kid in the face and telling him he was the result of a cheap truck-stop condom and a loofah sponge diaphragm. Somehow, telling them to cover up is assumed to be a gateway to suicide. And it's every girl—tall, short, fat, skinny, black, white, rich, poor—who wears them. I was sitting across from a very white, suburban-looking family at an airport recently (you know, the kind of family that "summers"). The daughter looked to be about fourteen. She was slender for her age, yet her shorts were tighter than Chris Brown's hands around a girlfriend's neck during a domestic dispute. They sat across from me, and as I glanced up, the girl was sitting with her legs a little too far apart. Either her shorts were too short, or her lady parts were just too darn long. More importantly, why did I, and the rest of the JetBlue customers, need to know she rolls commando? And why didn't her parents forbid her from wearing those in the first place? "Well, better to have creepy perverts publicly masturbating to our daughter than to tell her *no* and risk upsetting her."

Things have gotten so out of hand with people feeling no embarrassment over how they look or behave. They're mixing up acceptance for things we have no control over, such as our sexual orientation or race, with acceptance for acting like an uncouth monster. Is it acceptable to be gay? Yes. Straight? Yes. Vietnamese? Yes. Is it okay to walk into Baskin Robbins and sample all thirty-one flavors because your "palate is just so picky"? Um, fuck no! It's also not okay to put your feet up at the movies, molest your muffin on the subway (I'm talking about eating like a slob, but I realize that can mean something else—and that's not okay either!), or walk barefoot at a concert, in a restroom, or any other public place other than the beach.

Coddling people started getting out of hand over the last fifteen years. It started somewhat innocently to build kids' self-esteem, but it morphed into giving people delusional confidence in all their abilities, including their thoughts. Remember Caitlin Upton, the 2007 Miss Teen USA pageant contestant from South Carolina? Her response to a question from the pageant went viral. The host asked, "Recent polls have shown a fifth of Americans can't locate the US on a world map. Why do you think this is?" This was her actual response: "I personally believe that US Americans are unable to do so because, uh, some people out there in our nation don't have maps and, uh, I believe that our education, like such as in South Africa and, the Iraq, everywhere like such as, and I believe that they should—our education over here in the US should help the US, uh, or, should help South Africa and should help the Iraq, and the Asian countries, so we will be able to build up our future, for our children." Um, what? That's a perfect example of why we need to bring the swimsuit competition back. More walkie and less talky. It's also an example of a parent constantly saying, "Honey, you can be anything you want to be. You are so smart; you can do whatever you want." Uh, no! Hot chicks should use their mouths for what they were meant for (lip injections to stay hot enough for other people to tolerate them).

Look, there's nothing wrong with wanting people to feel good about themselves. But like most situations, too much of a good thing can be bad. A little bit of fried food is good. A triple cheeseburger topped with fries, onion rings, and fried twinkies cooked in lard could kill you. A little bit of country music on your iPhone is harmless. Too much, and you're involuntarily vetted into the Aryan Nation Brotherhood. A little bit of plaid with your prints is fashionable. Too much, and you're a Brooklyn hipster. Modesty is good, moderation is enough, and nothing good comes from excess other than Hall & Oates' music.

16

Demi's Not So Sweet N' Low-Key Meltdown

I was done writing this book, but then Demi Lovato had a meltdown over sugar-free options at the Bigg Chill yogurt shop in LA. They said they were triggered because it reminded them of diet culture, and as a bulimic, they didn't feel "safe." Excuse me, what? Some kids are terrified to go home because they have abusive parents. There are people in the military that worry they'll never see their loved ones again. Some women live in fear that their boyfriend may someday see them without makeup. And this stunod is tormented by a tasty frozen treat?

Lovato took to their Instagram story to let fans know they were triggered by the sugar-free options and accused the shop of "harmful messaging." So diabetics should have to *guess* which foods are safe for them? What about people with Celiac Disease? Should they keep those labels a mystery as well? If they shit their brains out, I guess that riddle will be solved. I empathize with the fact Lovato has mental health issues. But can you imagine believing that the world is supposed to predict and adjust every possible scenario that could set you off rather than you learning to adapt to potential triggering stimuli in your daily travels? What's next? Is Demi going to go to Gold's Gym (the other "#DietCulture-Vultures") and demand they get rid of the exercise equipment and only offer TVs and recliners? When you have the option to not go somewhere, but the only option you see is to storm in with your attitude and emotional support bee peeking out of your Chanel bag, please know that you need to tie your tubes and your hands, so you can't post these imagined mistreatments on social media. And if you're that easily triggered, throw away your guns, so you don't use those triggers on the rest of us. Thanks.

PART 3

DROPS of StUPidER

17

#YACHTCOCaiNEPROSTitUtEs aNd CHaD

You know what's funnier than a good joke: when people stomp off because they're offended by a joke. It's hilarious to observe a person overreact to something as unimportant as an attempt at humor. Case in point: A while back, trending on Twitter was #YachtCocaineProstitutes. Boom! Immediately, I start cracking up. I think it sounds like the name of an eighties rock band. So, I tweet, "Wow, I can't believe how much people are tweeting about my band #YachtCocaineProstitutes. They're touring with the slightly less popular #'87BuickSkylarkMethSkanks." Silly enough, right? Well, not according to Mad Chad (that's not his Twitter handle, but it should be.)

Chad replies to the tweet with, "I have to unfollow you now because of that tweet." First of all, my life fell apart in that instant. How could I go on without the support of Chad and his blurry profile picture that looks like it was taken underwater? That charming, perpetually confused looking jerks-off-to- Japanese-anime face would no longer be available to me. When he first followed me, I followed him back. But now, he was blocking me like an artery in his fat heart. Could I ever find joy again without seeing his retweets of everybody else's thoughts and none of his own? Boy, he showed me, didn't he? But wait? How could his block teach me a lesson when I don't even know what he was upset about?

I've heard of people flipping out over jokes with sensitive topics such as rape or murder. Years ago, I had a rape joke in my set. If you literally think I was making fun of rape itself, please stop reading now. Making fun of the scumbags who commit this atrocity is *not* making fun of rape. If you can't comprehend that . . . wait, why are you still reading? I told you to go away. Okay, back to the rape-joke story. An Uptighty Whitey stops me after a show and says how horrible that I made fun of rape.

"Do you know anybody who's been raped?" She thought she had me, but the fact was, I had a close friend who was raped . . . twice. And it ruined her life. That friend was a fan of my bit and understood the point of it. Meanwhile, this past-her-prime preppy pit bull was trying to explain to me why the bit was so offensive. The only problem was, she couldn't. Pressing her for why the bit was unacceptable, the best she could come up with was, "It's just wrong."

This is the problem with people who always have something to whine about. They're so busy whining, they can't hear anything else besides their own inner psychobabble. They don't listen to content; they just hear a word or phrase and zero in on it. In fact, I think some of these people are on high alert, just waiting for something they can take a stance on. So, they hear the word *retard*. They don't bother to listen to what's being said; they just know they're going to expose you for the scum that you are. Meanwhile, you're just discussing how a new medicine might retard the progression of a certain disease.

But back to Chad. Unless Chad's mom was run over by a slutty meth head in a stolen Skylark, I'm stumped as to what triggered Chad's Twitter tantrum. But he's just another person being an overly sensitive, dramatic whiner who can't handle something they disagree with—even if they don't even know what they disagree with. And how stunted is Chad if he thought that joke had any political connotation? Read the words, you defective, clueless sweatpants-at-church-wearing slob. Yachts, cocaine, and prostitutes (AKA "models" from South America who magically appear amongst perverted millionaires on the open sea) are considered toys of the rich. The trailer-trash version is a shitty car, low-end drugs, and chicks who bang for free. So, while the hashtag itself may have been affiliated with some political controversy, the joke was merely a play on words. But, if you're reading this book, I probably didn't need to spell that out for you. And if you're Chad, I'm sorry you have to fuck a sock.

18

KeePiNG Up WiTh thE KaRdOUChEians

You know what I hate more than *Keeping Up With the Kardashians*; myself, for watching enough episodes to be familiar with them. This is a family that takes the no shame in my game mentality to another level. Americans are so PC now and all about forcing their self-declared greatness on others that we've lost the ability to be embarrassed, feel shame, or maintain a sense of decorum (or a sense of décor. Why the hell are people still living with braided rugs and knick-knacks?). The Kardashians—or, as I call them, the Kar*douche*ians—represent what feels like an epidemic in this country. It's the epidemic of convincing yourself that nothing you do is shameful or worth hiding.

First, you have the mom, Kris Jenner, who's a pimp. She pimped out her daughter's sex tape for fame and money. Then she was married to Caitlyn Jenner before her transition and makeover to looking like Janet Reno with Cindy Crawford's to-die-for hair. It seems Kris married Jenner for fame. But even though she was an Olympic decathlete, it wasn't Caitlyn's limber legs and proficiency with a long pole that brought Kris the fame she seemed to crave. Turns out daughter Kim's pole skills were a little more marketable. Kim's the most famous of the Kardashians. She's most well-known for a "leaked" sex tape and an ass that looks like a sack of rotten yams. While everybody knows it's about as real as a certain Scientologist's interest in women, Kim thought she could convince the public otherwise by getting a "butt x-ray" to prove to the world there's never been anything foreign inside her ass. Upon closer examination, I'm sure that x-ray would reveal half the NBA, half the NFL, and all of

Ray J's relatives. But what does an x-ray on a TV show prove? And frankly, who gives a shit? The proof is in the curdled pudding, otherwise known as her ass fillers.

This has to be the most appalling family known to the public. They seem to pop babies out for sport and trot them around like accessories. Their parenting philosophy appears to be the more money we spend on the kid, the less time we actually have to be with it. They seem entirely oblivious to their inability to attract a decent partner in life. How many times do we have to watch poor, innocent Khloé's heart get broken by another sleazebag who nobody could've predicted would be up to shenanigans behind her back? [insert sarcastic shocked look here] Lamar Odom had the personality and exuberance of a turtle on a respirator. But that seems to be her type: Low energy guys who mumble when they speak. Maybe they can't muster the strength to talk because they're drained from banging prostitutes and Kylie Jenner's friends all night. No need to feel bad for Khloé, though. She chose to get knocked up by Tristan Thompson, who ("allegedly") had a girlfriend when she started seeing him. Oh, and that girlfriend was six months pregnant at the time.

Khloé used to be the likable one—if there could be such a thing in this wanton family. She seemed a little more down-to-earth, funny, and compassionate. But when she resorted to Kim-level plastic surgery, she altered her whole appearance and changed her personality to mirror Kim's dead-inside disposition. The only thing that awakens Kim's otherwise flat, emotionless tone is the chance to bully brother Rob, sister Kourtney, or Taylor Swift. Taylor is an accomplished singer-songwriter who plays guitar, piano, ukulele, and banjo. Kim plays the skin flute and the victim. Somebody whose claim to fame is spreading her legs and a seventy-two-day marriage sounds idiotic criticizing somebody who's famous for having enviable talents.

When I last watched a couple of years ago, Khloé became Kim's partner in vitriol. Together they berated and persecuted Kourtney. Kourtney, while not 100 percent natural, is still the prettiest and most natural-looking of the family. She has a genetically perfect butt and a face that resembles the one she had as a teen. Kim and Khloé, on the other hand, look like gangster Mdoka White Lip fish who got stuck in a tanning bed in a greasy wind tunnel. Kim told Kourtney she was "the least interesting to look at." If a naked Eva Mendes was standing next to a plane crash, she'd be the least interesting to look at too. It doesn't mean you want to jerk off to the crash. It just means it's hard to avert your eyes from disaster.

I think my favorite part of the episodes is when Kim and Kris talk to the cameras. They were obviously coached over the years to speak more quietly and deliberately to suggest some level of gentility. You can't chew gum like a cow while getting laid on video blabbering like a *Girls Gone Wild* reject and think you're classlessness can be softly spoken away. As the saying goes, "You can take the giant penis out of the girl's fake ass, but you can't take the ass injections out of the girl." I don't know. Something like that. No one in this clan has a respectable relationship, but that doesn't stop them from making kids in their unstable, temporary unions. Rob Kardashian thought it was reasonable to knock up a volatile stripper named Blac Chyna. She looks about four foot nine with six feet wide hips (turns out she's actually five foot two with seven feet wide hips). It's like a human funhouse mirror minus the fun. She's (allegedly) violent and abuses drugs and alcohol. In other words, the perfect candidate to create a life with. Khloé appears to be desperate for any guy who shoots hoops and shoots loads into other women while dating her. Kim married a man who thinks he's Jesus. But would Jesus write these lyrics, "... I impregnated your mouth girl. Ooooh, that's when I knew you could be my spouse girl"? Hmm, me thinks not.

People revere the Kardoucheians—a family who can be identified by their genitals and vocal fry. They're also known for their friendship with violent pervert, Joe Francis—a man whose own mother has a restraining order against him. He also has an impressive list of criminal charges including (but probably not limited to): false imprisonment, assault causing great bodily injury, and domestic violence. Remember when Americans admired TV families like *The Brady Bunch* and *Leave it to Beaver*? The Kardashians are more like *The Bawdy Bunch*. And if Kim ever wants her own spinoff with the kids, she can call it *Leave it to Mom's Beaver*.

19

PRay the GAY AWaY CamP

PRIEST: So your son has a sexual desire to be with other men?

PARISHIONER: Yes, Pastor Bill. He said he's had these urges since he was young.

PRIEST: I see. Well, I have good news. We've found that the most effective way to cure this affliction is to gather a group of men with the same feelings, send them to a secluded cabin in the woods, and give them lots of sweaty activities to do together that always end in a cuddle-huddle and group shower, all under the supervision of a curiously single "reformed," sexually charged, "celibate" man who hates pants. He can pray this sickness away.

PARISHIONER: Praise Jesus!

How the fuck are there people who actually believe you can send guys to a camp to pray their gay away? I know they do this to women too, but that's really just a YouPorn category you agree to peruse when you're trying to spice up your stale love life. But seriously, there are "conversion therapy" programs worldwide trying to shame men and women into being heterosexual. Knowing this is how some heterosexuals think, I'd rather be gay. If you can pray sexuality away, can I also pray away my short stature, left-handedness, uneven boobs, and my lack of desire to fondle children?

I enjoy people who say sexuality is a choice; because when you break that thought down, it really suggests we're all bisexual, but we *choose* which sex we'll have intimate relationships with. How can it mean anything else when a choice, by definition, is *the act of selecting or making a decision when faced with two or more possibilities*? Did you choose to be straight? Yeah, I'm talking to you, hetero reader! Did you one day say to your fourteen-year-old self, "Well, let's see. Bo Duke's ass looks like two delicious state-fair candy apples in those Wranglers . . . but . . . I'd love to wear Daisy Duke's legs like a necklace. Hmm, I guess I'll like women. But that Bo's ass . . . no, no . . . I choose women." Do you remember the day you *chose* to ignore your homosexual desires and *chose* heterosexuality instead, or did your penis choose for you the first time your sixth-grade teacher missed a button on her blouse?

Sexuality is no more a choice than height, color, or IQ. But if anti-gay proponents believe innate things are really a choice, are they saying they choose to be idiotic, braindead, robotic morons who can't think for themselves? Or is that just how God made them?

SLUTty TeRMS of ENdeaRMeNt

A few weeks ago, while getting some air outside of a comedy club between sets, I overheard some girls yelling and thought a fight broke out. One shouted from down the street, "Get over here bitch!" while pounding her chest like an enraged baboon. The other girl yelled back while giving the middle finger, "Shut up, you fucking slut!" Then they ran towards each other and hugged. They were using these words as terms of endearment. When I was in school, there was shame connected to being called a bitch or a slut, so we had to use codewords like *popular* or *cheerleader*.

Not only is there pride in these monikers now, but women mistakenly believe that calling themselves stupid names and discussing the moisture level of their genitals is a form of female empowerment. Take the song "WAP" for instance. It stands for wet-ass pussy. How is it empowering to tell your intended partner to bring a mop for the cleanup? Not only is that gross, but who the hell's looking to do janitorial work after a roll in the hay? Or ever? I must admit, though, I'm impressed that they knew to put the hyphen in *wet-ass*.

The dryer predecessor to "WAP" was "Bitch" by Meredith Brooks. Women in karaoke bars across America would courageously screech this ditty out while pointing at petrified horny men in the crowd. But at least bitches didn't get hassled. They seemed so angry that nobody wanted to find out if they had a WAP.

So the takeaway here is that if you call yourself a bitch or slut, you may or may not be one—but you're undoubtedly a numbskull.

LeadeR of the PACK ATTaCK

A pack attack is when people join the pack in hating something popular to hate without knowing why they hate it in the first place. The best example is a Nickelback Pack Attack. Hating Nickelback is a trendy vehicle to expose your self-believed coolness and convince people you're a deep thinker. Using them as a punchline to any joke—whether on stage or in a group of friends—guarantees laughter and lots of wide-eyed, "Oh snap!" fist-bump reactions. But why and how did they become the butt of the joke? The go-to fall guys for insults? I can't say that I like or listen to them, but I don't hate them. If I don't like an artist, I just move on. I don't stew about it and rue the day they hit it big. Why would I care? There are so many more fun things to hate (like ear stretching or Josh Duggar)!

People argue that they hate Nickelback because they don't deserve their level of fame. Then they'll express anger that a band they love is underappreciated. But the moment said underappreciated band catches on and makes it big, they hate them too and accuse them of selling out. This makes about as much sense as GILF porn.

Metallica also gets this venom from "fans." You may not care for the direction they took at certain times, but it reeks of eighth grade to hate a band because not every piece of music sounds identical. Creativity isn't predictable, can't be planned, and isn't always a home run. Sometimes you get stuck, and you try other things. Some of those things fail, and some grab a new audience. And sometimes you hire a YouTube singer to replace a legend and pretend you're not suddenly a cover band.

Hating someone for succeeding is senseless . . . unless they're succeeding at being a pedophile. That warrants hatred, as do the celebrities who gain success from fucking for fame but pretend it's just from hard work (in their defense, I imagine that fucking Harvey Weinstein was hard work). Although I don't listen to Nickelback, I am grateful for them. They allow people to identify who's cool—not based on your hatred of them, but by your indifference to them, or maybe even your fearlessness in admitting you like them. But my appreciation stems from the fact that we wouldn't have Sal Governale's parody of "Photograph." So I thank this Canadian conundrum for giving us something to ponder.

22

AiN't That Classy?

Ever notice that people who refer to things as classy aren't classy? Think of the intro to *Jersey Shore* that includes a sound bite of JWoww saying, "We're so classy now." This is a typical mistake made by people who suddenly come into money by way of meselthelioma lawsuits, scratch-off ticket winnings, or brawling on television sans underwear. They equate money with class. But class is how you conduct yourself, coupled with worldliness and sophistication that isn't found in a drunken stranger's crotch at a cheesy nightclub.

Rule number one of classiness is that it doesn't need to be declared; it just is. Rule number two is that if you speak the word classy, it shouldn't have a Wisconsin or Staten Island accent attached to it or the phrase *shit ton*. "Look at dat broad. She got a shit ton of class." In fact, it shouldn't have any accent attached to it unless it's British or Australian. You never have to point out or announce that something is classy. I understand this might confuse some people, so here's a simple test to figure out if you're not classy. Have you ever referred to a tattoo, strip club, or a quinceañera as classy? Case closed.

Years ago, a guy came up to me after a show. He explained how much he enjoyed my set and wished his girlfriend could've been there, but she was working. I asked where she worked, and he names some local strip club and adds, "But it's a classy strip club." I don't know about anybody else, but when I think of classy, I think five-star hotel or five-star restaurant, not five-*scar* dancer dragging her malnourished, meth-addicted body across the stage just to get a dollar from a domestic abuser with a lazy eye in an airbrushed *Myrtle Beach '98* muscle shirt. You know what would be classy? How about a Zamboni to clean the stage between dancers? Or Lysol bombs detonated every twenty minutes in the club to sanitize the copious amounts of baby batter all over the chairs, tables, floors, and dollar bills. But it's better on inanimate objects than in an actual person I suppose. Babies being conceived in strip clubs is never classy. At least wait until your dancer is on break and do it in your van.

23

If YOU UNLOCK It, THey WiLl ComE...
and KiLL YOU, You Big DuMmy

I watch many shows on the ID (Investigation Discovery) channel, and I always wonder two things: How does everyone live in a town where they don't have to lock their doors, and who the heck is Maureen Maher's stylist? She's a human mullet. She's leathered up on top with genitals-absent slacks below. It's like a party on the top and sex only on birthdays and anniversaries on the bottom.

The narration on these true crime shows always starts the same way: "Possumneck, Mississippi is a small, tight-knit community where people don't lock their doors. With a population of three people—the victim, the killer, and a five and dime owner/pastor/selectman/sheriff/electrician—Possumneck was never a hotbed of crime, other than a meth epidemic . . . and round-the-clock domestic dispute calls . . . and a moonshine ring . . . and an embezzling church secretary. So how would anyone ever figure out who killed Tammy-Jo Johnson?"

I never watched one of these shows where the crime wasn't in a "safe" suburban or rural community lined with unlocked houses. The show never starts out like, "Camden New Jersey is fucking scary. Most residents have six deadbolts on their door, five pit bulls, and a good reason to be suspicious of who's on the other side of the door. So, who broke into Ray Ray's joint and jacked his shit?" Do you know why those shows never start like that? Because city people are smart. They know to lock up their shit and not trust every turdbag that happens to have the same zip code as them.

What the hell kind of mentality is that? "Well, golly gee. Ted Bundy from down the road once brought candied yams to a church pot-luck, so I guess that means he's a trustworthy fella, and I don't have to lock my doors."

The super wacko crimes are almost always committed by white people in the suburbs. You never hear of a black handyman who thinks he's Jesus crawling into a second-story window to abduct a child for "religious" purposes while his subservient wife dutifully helps shackle their intended love slave. White women will blindly obey a smelly, crazy-eyed, self-proclaimed prophet wearing a filthy t-shirt as shorts, but no black woman is going along with that crap. She'd be like, "You're a sick fuck. I ain't down with that shit. Get the fuck outta here, you creepy, sick-ass bitch muthafucka."

So the moral of the story is: when a realtor tells you it's a "safe neighborhood" where you "don't have to lock your doors and every-body knows your name," run like hell to the closest city where no one gives a fuck about welcoming you, and start picking out names for your newly acquired pet pit bull after your order a Yosemite Sam "Back Off" *un*welcome mat on Etsy.

24

The Dumb Jury's In: Even if it Fits, They'll Still Acquit

I got called to jury duty last week. Wow! Have you ever seen what shows up there? Nobody there appears particularly savvy, astute, or from this planet. Where do they find these people? They look like they crawled out from under a rock. Can you imagine being the victim of a crime, and justice is in the hands of a group of people who still haven't figured out it's not normal to need dentures by the age of twenty-three?

People are so stupid they don't even understand what *reasonable doubt* means. Take the Casey Anthony jurors. They had plenty of evidence: chloroform-stained rags, the odor of a dead body in the trunk, false statements, computer searches for foolproof suffocation methods, and **THE BABY'S BODY WRAPPED IN BEDDING FROM THE HOME WITH DUCT TAPE OVER HER MOUTH!** They let her walk free because, as one juror stated, "We know she wasn't innocent, but we couldn't find her guilty." Shithead says what?

They think reasonable doubt means allowing room for any proposed scenario (no matter how preposterous) other than the most logical one—putting *possibility* over probability. So those paint lickers let a child murderer off. "Well, we can't prove that aliens didn't come to take the child. And wait a minute. There's also a picture of mom smiling with her daughter. She couldn't have done it." That's like saying Carson Kressley isn't gay if he wears a pair of Wranglers and gets drunk at a roadhouse in Lubbock, Texas, while espousing about "them damn homos" before heading home to punch his scrapbook-making wife in the face for asking why he's late again. Earth to jurytards: It's not like there's going to be a picture of her dosing her daughter with Xanax ("say *cheese!*") before chloroforming her while doing a thumbs up and tossing her in a trunk.

While jurytards have been around forever, they mostly flew under the radar until exploding onto the scene in 1995. When OJ Simpson was found not guilty of murder because he put a pair of shrunken leather gloves on, over rubber gloves, with swollen fingers (after purposely discontinuing his arthritis medication before the trial started), it set a new precedent for stupidity. The inability to comprehend the term *reasonable doubt* has benefitted quite a few killers (e.g. George Zimmerman, Amanda Knox, Robert Durst, Kyle Rittenhouse). Proof beyond a reasonable doubt doesn't mean proof to an absolute certainty. For example, I know that guys with fake tans and Louis Vuitton accessories are total tool bags despite not having DNA evidence (such as a rag with their crusty hair gel on it). I have to go by photos and patterns of behavior to convict on overwhelming circumstantial evidence: running hand down own abs while dancing at a wedding with sunglasses on, looking like eastern European club bouncers with tiny bangs shellacked to their foreheads while wearing giant gold necklaces and jeans with offensively large red stitching (or velour tracksuits), trying to look pensive in mirror-selfies while really just looking confused, shaving all their body hair to make sure the crucifix tattoo is properly displayed, and calling pasta sauce *gravy*.

We need a new questionnaire that can quickly eliminate people who have no business making important decisions. And this questionnaire can also double as a tool to determine if you should be allowed to vote.

—— What grade were you in when your first child was born?

—— Do you have a ponytail . . . and a penis . . . and an AARP card?

—— Have you ever seen the image of Jesus or the Virgin Mary in a tree trunk, an ashtray, or your Denver omelet?

—— Have you ever worn a jean jacket and jeans . . . at the same time?

Dismissed.

Adult Babies

Whether it's the grownups who complain about every wrong that's ever been done to them or the ones who like to sit in a giant high-chair while being fed a ba-ba by a loner from a fetish site, they're both terrible. Add in Bronies (adult men who are fans of the *My Little Pony* TV show) and grownups who refuse to eat vegetables (that aren't deep-fried and/or slathered in Crisco), and you're looking at the results of what happens when Walmart shoppers are allowed to reproduce.

As children, we don't have choices or control. As adults, we do. So if you had an atrocious childhood but somehow survived, stop torturing yourself by living in yesterday and acting like you're eternally two. The only person you're punishing is yourself by being a self-imposed victim. The best "fuck you" is to live a decent life instead of demanding braces from your mom when you're forty-two because she didn't get them for you when you were twelve. Now go grab your therapy ostrich, get out of the past, put down your Grand Theft Auto headset, stop blaming everybody but yourself for where you are now, treat yourself to the asthma inhaler your parents deprived you of, and live while you're alive.

"Don't Judge"

Don't judge? Really? If I see a twat with hair extensions in a Range Rover taking up two spaces, someone in *Camp Auschwitz* attire, a 40-year-old dude wearing a *Team Britney** shirt, or an adult sniffing their fingers, I'm fucking judging.

*For the record, I'm Team Britney

PART 4

I'm SO OVARY YOU

27

ANdREa NewmAN

Growing up, I tried to get along with everyone and never concerned myself with being in a certain crowd. The fact that no particular group was clamoring for my membership may have also influenced my involuntary decision not to be in one. I always knew cliques were for dicks, so it worked out well that I didn't seem to qualify for any. Instead, I told bawdy jokes (not knowing what they meant or what *bawdy* meant) and did impressions of my male teachers. There's nothing like a ten-year-old girl in pigtails swatting a yardstick and coughing up faux phlegm balls. While it didn't get me invited to any dances or parties, it did carry me through to middle school.

My inimitable yet unrelatable behavior was intriguing enough to attract the stragglers who weren't "cool" enough for the popular crowd and not smart enough for the nerds. In seventh grade, I became close friends with one such straggler named Sasha Winston. We hung out the entire school year, but when summer break started, she disappeared faster than Nick Cannon's condoms at a Diva's of Soul concert . . . or a *Wild 'N Out* meet and greet . . . or Red Lobster after Sunday service.

Sasha discovered Andrea Newman that summer. Ah, Andrea—the cliché, middle-school preppy douche (she was like a human bottle of Summer's Eve with tiny whales all over it). Andrea was one of those kids who, even at fourteen, looked like a forty-five-year-old suburban housewife. In other words, she looked like a man. If you didn't know any better, you might've called her a broad-shouldered, chiseled-chin hunk. I mean, she had all the trappings of a male heartthrob: that Ted Koppel cavalier-attitude-toward-finding-a-part hairdo, Kelly-green wide wale cords, and a Fair Isle sweater strategically tied around her never-been-kissed neck. She was Stan Gable (*Revenge of the Nerds*) with darker hair and smaller boobs. Andrea always matched from head to toe. Not only did her clothing match perfectly, but she was so coordinated that her personality even matched her looks: she was as ugly on the inside as she was on the outside. Poor little fella.

During that summer, I got a letter in the mail from Sasha and the stuck-up titan of tools, Andrea. Sasha and Mandrea weren't friends during the school year, but Sasha was so desperate to be in with the rich kids, she must've spent the entire summer kissing Andrea's concave ass and spit-shining her penny loafers. So I get this letter that said something to the effect of, "Claudia, you are such a loser. Nobody wants to be friends with you because you're poor, and you live in an apartment with your divorced mother who has no money." It was proudly signed, "Very Preppily Yours, Andrea, and Sasha."

Granted, everything they said was true. I was poor (probably because I was an unemployed child. Unless somebody was looking for a hairy, underage Pat Benatar stand-in, I didn't have any potential work on the horizon), and I did live in an apartment with my husband-less mother. But how, and more importantly, why, were they so knowledgeable about my mom's love life and financial status? What happy fourteen-year-old kid is obsessed with (let alone even aware of) a thirty-six-year-old woman's personal life? Did she meet my mom on a field trip and sniff out her Jean Naté drugstore perfume, "Eww, Claudia's mom can't afford Enjoli; she must live in (gasp) an apartment!" Could I even afford to partake in a field trip? The abstruseness of these quandaries was beyond my skill set. Until this point, the most investigative work I had done was hunting down a Japanese edition of *Tiger Beat* that revealed what Steve Perry did to get his hair so shiny. (Turns out, sweating profusely on stage isn't really a beauty secret.)

I guess I was a loser because they seemed to know more about my mom than I did. What kind of a daughter was I not to realize how poor or how divorced my mom was? All the signs were there, but I must've been blind to think transportation via a 1976 Gremlin with hand-crank windows was all the rage (and even blinder not to realize it was the source of Sasha and Andrea's rage). They forgot to mention that I was also an idiot. How could I not know that my mother's marital status determined the number and quality of friends I should have?

Gosh, I was stupid. It was true, I was a poor child of a divorcée, but at least I wasn't a wuss. This was an era when bullying was done in person, but these two wimps opted to hide behind pen and paper. And if you're going to scribe a hate letter, at least inject some pizazz into your write-rage. One thing's for sure, neither of them was a Sylvia Plath . . . and that's unfortunate because Sylvia Plath killed herself.

Can you imagine a couple of guys wasting time writing a letter like that to another guy? "Dear Bobby, we ain't gonna be seen witchu no more cuz it's recently come to our attention that your dad drives a Hyundai and smells like old socks. That ain't cool, and neither are you. Fondly, Rick and Eddie." Of course, that would never happen because 1) Hyundais aren't as embarrassing as they were in 1984, and 2) guys don't give a crap about what their friends do, what their friends' parents do, or where they live.

And based on my example, I don't think Rick and Eddie could write even if their fingers were Bic pens. Guys just want friends to eat, drink, and look at boobs with. Drunkenness doesn't feel any different with money, and boobs look good no matter what tax bracket you're in. Guys don't write assaultive breakup letters to other guys. If something's bothering them, they just say it to your face—or they write rambling manifestos, grab a Red Bull, and spend all night designing their costume for the next Furry convention.

The point is: what reason other than jealousy could prompt such a nasty attack? I had to question the validity of this letter, though. Why would somebody so happy with their own circumstances write a letter like that? If being the child of wealthy parents was so great, and I was such an insignificant loser, why was I having such an impact on these girls' lives? Before receiving that letter, I was barely aware of Sir Prep-A-Lot, so why was I on her radar? No matter how I looked at it, it always came back to jealousy. What were they jealous of, you ask? Maybe the fact that I didn't need a blow dryer to feather my hair, it just happened naturally. Perhaps it was because I didn't have to look like one of the guys to be one of the guys. Maybe it was the fact I wore a half-zip, midnight-blue, velour Izod shirt like nobody's business. I don't have the answers; I can only speculate. And I can only speculate that Andrea was no longer a big fish in a little pond when she transferred to private school. She was probably a little microscopic whale on some big chinos.

28

YOU MUST LoVe

The MaRVeLoUS MRS. MaiSEL

You know what I hate more than *The Marvelous Mrs. Maisel*? When a person finds out I'm a comedian and follows it up with, "You must love *The Marvelous Mrs. Maisel*!" It's like assuming that every UPS driver loves *The King of Queens* and dressing like a human poop emoji. Why must I love this show? Do people presume that *all* comedians love this show, or just the ones with vaginas?

But since I never actually watched it, I thought maybe I was being close-minded, so I watched a best-of montage of Maisel's stand-up. If that's the best, I'm glad I never tuned in for the rest. I even watched—okay, *tried* to watch— "20 Badass Moments," from Buzzfeed videos. I understand the story is set in a different era, but it could easily be used as a hackney handbook. Again, I ask, why "must" I love this show? Because I'm a female comic? There are so many styles of comedy, yet people think being a woman is a style. Maybe that's because some female comics beat to death the same tired topics about how good it is to find a *hard* man but how hard it is to find a good man [*insert calamitous dating stories here*], how their kids are driving them up a wall ("Chianti, take me away, and add a little CBD oil!"), and how women are smarter than men. If they're so bright, why are they always dating and marrying men they think are dumb? And don't get me wrong; I'm not against female comedians. Joan Rivers, Nikki Glaser, and Natasha Leggero are some of my favorite comics—not *female* comics; just comics.

That's my point. I'm into people who make me laugh *regardless* of their privates. Funny is funny.

The show may be well-written, well-produced, and well-acted, but it's a snoozer for me. And just because the show is about a comedian doesn't make it a comedy! Maybe I would've been more receptive if it wasn't being touted as a comedy. Gee, what a hoot to watch a woman struggle with marital issues while trying to make it in a male dominated industry as she gets shit on like Johnny Depp's bed. This isn't a comedy! It's a drama. Do you know what else is full of drama? Broads, chicks, dames, gals. I can prove that statement right now. If you're a woman who just read that remark and you're seething, I give you exhibit A.

Relax. It's a joke. And just like *Maisel*, it's not that funny.

29

The View

The View doesn't do anything to dispel the stereotype that some women are yammering nags who can't let anything go and believe that screaming the loudest makes your point the most valid. Remember when your mom, wife, or girlfriend would rant and rave at you until you just agreed so she would shut the hell up? Did you ever think, "Now, if only I could have that more often but with four moms and wives at once"? That's what *The View* is. The end.

30

PReTtY FUNny

Why do people assume a woman's shallow or unfunny if she doesn't fill out a pair of khakis like Jake from State Farm? I believe you should never judge a person by their beauty or their size. You should always judge them by their religion and income bracket. Sheesh. Everybody knows that! If you got pissed at that, this book isn't for you. Oh, and you should also judge a person by their ability to take—and recognize—a joke. It's like taking a punch in the face—only more pleasant (unless you happen to be into s&m).

Several years ago, a fellow comedian booked me for eight minutes of stage time on a show he produced with a female comic named Julia (No, that's not her real name, but you know who you are, Jerky Julia). Shows like that tend to have multiple comics on the bill (hence the short time for a set). So I show up at the club, and Julia's standing there, but her partner Jeff isn't. I tell her my name and let her know that Jeff booked me for the show. She looks me up and down and tells me she doesn't have me on the list. Then she says, "We don't usually let skinny bitches on the show, but if Jeff booked you, I'll allow it." Huh? Did she just attack me for no reason other than my size? And indirectly tell me that she discriminates against women whose bellies aren't larger than their tits? I hoped she was just joking with a hack, cliché line overused by rotten, unoriginal, bagel-faced women (and no, that's not an anti-Semitic jab. It literally means her face looked like a misshapen bread product). But she wasn't kidding.

Soon after that weird intro, the herd of comics was corralled into the room where the show takes place. She refused to let me know where I was in the lineup, but one after the other, each comic does a minimum of eight minutes. Finally, she tells me I'm up next but says I can only do three minutes. I remind her that Jeff booked me for eight, but she reiterates, "Three. That's it." So now I have to blow through a set at the same rate she demolishes crab Rangoon at an all-you-can-eat buffet. I'm on stage for two minutes when she gives me the light. I was so confused because I knew I hadn't gotten to two and a half minutes yet. So I look at her again, and she's giving me the signal to get off the stage as in "now!" I knew I'd never do that show again, so I ignored her demand and finished my three minutes. When I thanked the crowd, they were yelling for me to keep going. She shot me a nasty look (also known as her face), so I respectfully left the stage. I wanted to punch her in her outdated vagina when she snatched the mic from me. I got more laughs than anybody else, yet she didn't want to give me stage time because I was a "skinny bitch." Slighting someone because of their looks is just as sleazy as providing them preferential treatment because of them.

That wasn't the first time I dealt with that mentality from a fellow comic or audience member. I did a show once where I got on stage and immediately noticed a table of eight scowling women planted front and center. In their defense, maybe they just ate the white-trash baked ziti that every comedy fundraiser promotes as "Italian dinner included in the ticket price!" There was only one woman seated at the table who laughed during my set. She came up to me afterward and said, "I just want you to know I wasn't with them. I came by myself, and that's where I was seated. I thought you were hilarious, but when you came out, the other women at the table said, "Ugh, who does this bitch think she is?" They assumed I couldn't be funny since I didn't have housewife hips and the "hilarious" stressed-mommy vibe.

Some comics have told me how hard it is for a woman like me (whatever that means) to be accepted in comedy, but they'd be "happy to help." But they made it difficult, if not impossible, for me to work at certain clubs when I wouldn't "play ball" (or play *with their* balls). There's no HR person to report this behavior to, and nobody gives a shit because the story's not big enough. Who's our Harvey Weinstein? Some dude that books Krazee's Comedy Club in a Ramada in South Dakota? A guy who's working the Comedy Cellar seven nights a week just so he can brag that he eats at a special table with a bunch of bald fatsos who baste each other's wieners with over-the-top psychotic laughter? (Don't get me wrong. If I were invited to join them, I would.)

A comic I was friendly with, Willie Fistagash, posted a picture on Facebook of four pretty comics and chastised them for getting stage time because of their looks. He wanted everybody to hate them for being good-looking, and he was backing it up with an assumption—rather than a fact—that they weren't funny. Even if they got stage time based on their looks, shouldn't he be pissed at **the bookers** rather than the girls? Why not post a picture of the bookers to humiliate them instead? Meanwhile, Willie produces a weekly show that looks like a MILF-porn casting call. Ninety percent of the comics on the show are female. And they're chicks whose looks far outweigh their comedic abilities. Yet, he's trying to humiliate these girls he doesn't even know by saying they're taking stage time from "real comics"? This is a guy who posts what he deems to be deep thoughts on social media. He wants people to know not only is he funny, but he's also caring and has all of you figured out. He's woke with jokes. He also repeatedly messaged me to get together despite explaining that I can barely function most days because of my health condition. Not getting to his Facebook messages quickly enough was another issue. He finally unfriended me for always being unavailable and posted a passive-aggressive post about bitchy comedians who don't do the dutiful "hanging out" that's expected of them. For somebody purporting to be so caring, he certainly didn't have an issue cutting me loose simply for being too ill to run around like Bella Hadid at a dirty-musician fair.

So what's the takeaway? Do women in comedy get more work for being attractive, or do they get punished before getting a chance to show their talents? All I know is that if I ever succumbed to giving some loser a blowjob for stage time, I'd smack it a few times, asking, "Is this thing on?" before finishing with an aggressive mic drop.

Chick Flick Schtick

When's the last time you were home alone on a Saturday night making baked goods and suddenly belted out a song into a wooden spoon wearing your Aquaman undies? Oh, and got caught by your secret crush, who you're otherwise invisible to except when he needs advice on the stuck-up bitch he's dating? This is Romantic Comedies 101. The protagonist is always a goofball, tomboy, or Rachel McAdams—and she has to snort when she laughs. But, for some reason, the superhot guy she's pining for is friends with her despite her quirky awkwardness. And he thinks she has all the answers to relationships even though she's never been in one, and he doesn't see her in a sexual way at all.

She has tits like torpedoes and a pillowy pout that's been entirely concealed by . . . a pair of glasses? Um, sure, okay. So, he's never noticed what a stacked babe (ahem, I mean, great person) she really is, but he's about to find out! Bitch-girlfriend (aka Whitney, Ashley, or Amber) just stormed off their date because he got her pink roses instead of red, so he comes running to nerd friend Jess and stops dead in his tracks when he catches a glimpse of her in the window adorably twerking to "Walking on Sunshine" . . . sans glasses! (Magically, she's got 20/20 when reading recipes). Coincidentally, the moment he sees her rack bouncing around like two delectable dodge balls is the moment he realizes what a good person she is and that love is about what's on the inside. Uh oh, is he going to work on things with Whiny Whitney or pursue Jiggly Jess? We all know Jess wins in the end because good prevails over evil (and hot guys love reclusive girls who hide their goods in baggy Pac-Man t-shirts . . . *snort, snort*). But, has this ever happened in real life? Do people really just "risk it all" because some dope cut loose in her kitchen wearing little boys' underwear?

Any rom-com worth its weight in clichés will include the airport scene or something equivalent. This is saved for the movie's end when the great guy (if he's so great, why is he always dating a C U Next Tuesday?) realizes he has to stop his true love (nerdy friend) from heading to Paris for art school. For some reason, they're great friends, but he didn't know she was moving to another country until their chubby immature jokester friend (Bobby) says, "She's on her way to the airport now!" with his big meatball eyes. Panic sets in, and the great guy (Jake) navigates all sorts of obstacles and potential calamities on his way to stop her from getting on the plane. Oh no! How is this going to turn out? Is she going to tell him he had his chance and she's going to ménage à trois her way through France? Or, will she melt at the sight of him sprinting across the gate to get to her and toss a promising life aside so she can live in middle America popping out babies while Jake develops a drinking problem playing pool every Friday night with the boys? More importantly, how the hell did he get through security?

Not every chick flick centers around a platonic friendship that blossoms into love. Sometimes it's the wrong place/wrong time scenario. This usually starts with an accidental meeting that involves being in a rush and important papers flying everywhere. Now she's pissed because she's on her way to an appointment, and this idiot bumped into her, but wait . . . their eyes meet as they kneel to pick up the mess, and she's lost in his baby blues. But it's not to be. She's engaged to a corporate stiff who keeps her soft side at bay.

Meanwhile, she keeps running into the clumsy free spirit she can't get out of her head. She finally sees the light, breaks it off with her guy, and plans to tell the clumsy stranger she wants to give it a go. But whoa, whoa, whoa, stop the clock! Now *he's* seeing somebody. Will the timing ever be right for these two mismatched soulmates? Probably not without the help of the leading lady's promiscuous, bespectacled pal who happens to practice witchcraft.

No rom-com would be complete without the heartbreaking misunderstanding. This is when the otherwise pragmatic gal will follow her heart and decide she will tell the guy that she does, in fact, have feelings. Unfortunately, her timing couldn't be worse. She walks into his apartment (because movie people never lock their doors—nor do any crime victims in Investigation Discovery documentaries) and finds him in a precarious position (reverse cowgirl) with his ex. Turns out, she decided to head over the same night his ex-girlfriend drugged him and is in the process of raping him. (They don't call it rape in rom coms. It's just an empowered, cute horny girl figuring out how to get what she wants. Somehow that's adorable). The "it's not what it looks like" scene takes shape with a close-up of the hurt gal's face welling up with tears. She doesn't want to hear his explanation, and he doesn't call the cops (which would probably make his rape claim a little more plausible to Sobbing Sally).

With so many clichés to choose from, I probably should highlight one of the worst. A girl has a little too much to drink, the guy is attracted to her, doesn't take advantage of her, instead takes care of her. What, what [*double head turn*]? That's about as realistic as Jimmy Fallon's laugh.

The thing I hate the most about chick flicks: I get sucked in. I end up watching them on a stormy Sunday, snowy Saturday, or any other day I can make a weather-related alliteration. Damn you, menstrual Mondays!

32

WhO's THE BoSs BItCH?

If you're one of those people who loves your job, go suck a bullet. Whoop-de-doo! I bet you like your neighbors too. My first adult job was at Fleet Bank. Nothing like naming a financial institution after an enema. "We'll have you shitting money in no time!" I was a customer service rep in an office full of women. Most of them were nice to me, but I attribute that to being unattractive enough for them to feel unthreatened. I couldn't even get my weight into the three digits back then, and my eyebrows looked like two John Oates mustaches. They had no idea what was lurking beneath my three-sizes-too-big suits (I had no idea I could have them altered rather than looking like a castoff from *Annie*).

I figured out how to dress when I transferred to a new bank. My improved appearance didn't go over well with the gals. I was rocking pencil skirts and fitted blazers like Anne Hathaway in *The Devil Wears Prada*, except I wasn't wearing Prada, I wasn't tall and striking, and my hair looked like I styled it while skydiving. But when you have a friendly personality, a sense of humor, and an appearance that doesn't look like dehydrated fruit, some women will hate you. I was popular with the customers because of my welcoming and considerate demeanor (my boss regularly received glowing letters about me from customers). Still, coworkers made my life hell with constant attempts to harass me. Bev was one of the managers who tried to forbid me from wearing my stylish skirts. She even went as far as to pretend a customer complained about my appearance. When I pressed for details, and she said it was a *male* customer, I knew she was full of crap. I called her on it, and she cracked. Bev, by the way, used to bring her parrot to work and limp around with it on her shoulder. Aye, aye Cap'n Cunt.

After repeated harassment from the pirate of pensions, I quit and became a claims adjuster at an insurance company. My male coworkers and field adjusters were easy to talk to and made me feel comfortable anytime I needed help. Unfortunately, my two department managers weren't as kind. Sharon looked like Larry Bird with Farrah Fawcett's hair if it were singed by a blowtorch. She also had the longest, flattest ass I've ever seen. You know how some women have an ass that doesn't quit? Sharon's couldn't quit because it never clocked in. Melinda looked like a shit brick house minus the brick and the house. She always commented on my body. Melinda had no problem reminding me of my flaws, often saying things like, "Geez, you're so skinny. Do you even weigh 100 pounds?" "Have a sandwich!" "If you turn sideways, you'll disappear." Occasionally, she added a "cutie" to make it appear innocent at the end of her attacks. But putting a bow on a knife you stabbed somebody with doesn't make the jabs duller.

I picked up on the job quickly, but they were suddenly unavailable anytime I had a question for either of them. They wanted me to fail just like their hair and fashion-sense had failed them. The average number of claims per day per adjuster was four. We just went through a major storm, so we started getting around thirty-two claims per day. It was impossible to keep up. Sharon and Melinda used this as an opportunity to accuse me of not doing my job. They screamed at me in front of the entire department that I wasn't doing enough. My coworker Jay stood up for me and said he was getting the same number of claims, yet only able to get to a fraction like me. That didn't stop their mission. They also told some male field adjusters to lie about what I did on specific files.

Did they really think these guys' loyalties would lie with two bitter buffoons or a friendly girl who learned faster than ninety percent of her peers and who could drop a pencil and bend over to pick it up like nobody's business? The abuse continued, so I quit and sued for harassment. I won. Eventually, I left the corporate world and began my comedy career thinking I'd gain more acceptance. Turns out, I'm even a misfit among oddballs, and bending over to pick up pencils doesn't really woo a crowd unless you're an elephant.

33

The GiRL NEXt Door...

to ThE PLastic SURGEoN

Remember when the girl next door was just an overly hyped, underwhelming object of American worship by men who never ventured more than twenty-five miles outside of their hometown? The Girl Next Door was the one at the bar you'd go *really?* when a group of thirty-year-old men in bucket hats and Third Eye Blind t-shirts would go, "Dude, she is so hot" as she chugged brewskis faster than Takeru Kobayashi inhales hot dogs. Guys referred to her as "the real deal" because she didn't' seem to fuss over hair, makeup, fashion, or alcoholism. The Girl Next Door didn't stand out in a crowd—she was neither stunning nor hideous—and she usually smelled like Dove soap because perfume was just too high maintenance for this victor of simplicity. The Girl Next Door of years-gone-by was referred to as relatable, down-to-earth, natural, and every other code word for *non-threatening to other women* because she was the human version of Wonder Bread. She was plain and familiar, yet endlessly enjoyable, and not likely to cause diarrhea.

What we now call the Girl Next Door is a completely different animal. Actually, more Frankenstein than animal since she's created in a medical setting . . . or spa . . . or a kitchen in the Bronx if you're trying to get it done on the cheap. It never occurs to these people that a woman named Guadalupe injecting you with a turkey baster as you stare at a velvet Jesus painting on the wall might not be an accredited plastic surgeon. And they're never embarrassed to file a lawsuit when their ass starts to look like a totaled car because the "filler" in their butt turns out to be tile grout and cement. Here's a tip: if your surgeon's name doesn't end in -*stein*, -*berg*, -*man*, or -*witz*, they're not a doctor!

Celebrities are the worst at pretending to be genuine girls next door and will blatantly lie to their fans. They do commercials for anti-wrinkle creams purporting to be astonished by the results and want us to believe we can all get the same outcome from a jar of hyaluronic acid and pig-placenta rather than from a Beverly Hills doctor who wears skinny jeans and Yeezy slides. The only reason so many of them can say, "I tried Botox once but it wasn't for me," with a straight face is because they literally have a straight face. Their faces don't move and their eyes are in a perpetual state of surprise. Maybe they're surprised that there's an astronomical number of dummies who believe them. The move they use to make themselves seem honest and relatable to fans is to do an interview or make an IG video to "reveal" that they "tried" Botox "once" but it wasn't for them. They usually add, "I'm an actress. My face has to be able to show expressions" as they struggle to speak through their Chiclet veneers, Daffy Duck lips, and tits up to their chins that look like Iggy Azalea's ass cheeks. But still, people believe that these women are all-natural. Guys say these present-day girls next door are hot because they're "low maintenance"—clearly clueless what they do just to appear as if they've done nothing. In today's world, there's no such thing as a genuine girl next door because these procedures start while they're still in school. Parents sign off on their kids getting this stuff done. Imagine looking like a Real Housewife at your first communion. Better keep the wine away from them!

I remember a guy once saying to me, "Wow! That looks like a lot of work. You must be high maintenance," as he pet my curls like I was a show poodle. That's how gullible guys are. I'm wearing my hair in its natural state because I can't be bothered (or trusted) with a piping hot iron to make my hair look silky and sexy, yet he thinks *I'm* the one who's high maintenance? Don't get me wrong, I'm just bitter because I can't participate in all the "treatments" these women do. If I didn't have a shit ton of allergies and self-esteem, I'd have that poison shot right into my face and get bangs to hide the one eye that can't close or blink as a result of it. "Yes honey, *that's* why I look so different. I got a new 'do." I can barely commit to a year of antivirus software, never mind risking my life every ten years to have my tits sliced open for a replacement set. I can't even remember to change my HVAC filter every six months. The girl next door is no longer the innocent girl with braids and freckles in a gingham check jumper. That's just a chick with a weird fetish. So let's just agree to call these gals the Girl Next Door with a little wink from our one unfrozen eye and already-raised eyebrow.

34

Vagisil Val

The first time I did stand-up was very similar to the first time I had sex: It wasn't very exciting, people looked confused, someone ended up blogging about me, and I got crabs (clearly, I had no idea how to use a microphone. And neither did the person before me).

Around 2004, a friend of mine was dabbling in stand-up. I'd been working up the nerve to get out there too, so when he mentioned he was heading to an open mic, I decided to give it a shot. I was told I'd get five minutes of stage time. A lot of open mic comics bring a cheat sheet on stage with them. I was proud of myself that for the very first time I'd be performing, I didn't need a piece of paper (sometimes I need a cheat sheet when I'm "performing" other things—but that usually doesn't involve an audience, a long electrical cord and an introduction using a fictitious name. *Usually*.). I thought that not using a cheat sheet gave me the appearance of seeming professional and prepared. What open mic host wouldn't give me kudos for that? Apparently, this one. I should mention that there are two types of comics running open mics: The big fish in a little pond (who smells like a fishy pond) and heavyset chicks with "nerdy ironic" glasses and purple streaks in their hair who overuse *LOL*.

The one running this open mic was a combination of both. Okay, I have no idea what she smelled like, but I imagine it couldn't have been good since her set mainly was about her need for Vagisil and her father bringing home "vats" of it for her. Personally, I didn't find the humor in this, but it certainly didn't evoke feelings of disdain towards her or her weight. Instead, I courteously laughed, listened, and waited for my turn.

Getting on stage, I was anxious. This was my first time, and I had no idea what to expect (besides nervous diarrhea). Aside from sounding a little scripted and not making enough eye contact (oh wait, am I talking about my first time again?), I did pretty well. At least I thought I did. When Vagisil Val came back to the stage, she ripped the mic out of my hands, gave me a stern look, and then made some comment to the crowd aimed at insulting me. She also said something to the effect of "not a good idea to make fun of fat people when a fat person is giving you stage time." Her remark was about a joke I made. The gist of the joke was pointing out the hypocrisy that people think it's okay to make fun of skinny people but not fat people. I never actually made fun of fat people. I shared my story of being accused of anorexia by a complete stranger and pointed out that it would never be okay for someone to accuse me of an eating disorder had I been fat.

The real hypocrisy was when she criticized me for making that point and insulted me for being skinny. To top it off, she brought a male comic to the stage after me who not only used the word fat but did so with disgust. He used physical gestures to illustrate how fat people waddle and walk like elephants and how their footsteps sound like earthquakes. Do you know what she did about this? She LAUGHED! The whole time he was up there, she was giggling like a horny hyena. When he was through, she hugged him, complimented him, and unknowingly reminded me why I have very few female friends.

I thought that was the end of it until my friend told me that Vagisil Val blogged about me the next day. She called me a skinny bitch, anorexic, and every other cliché about thin chicks. Obviously, there are many types of jokes and many types of comedy. If you're a comic, you don't have to think everything is funny, but you should at least have a sense of humor and not take yourself so seriously. Oh, and laughing burns calories. Maybe Val should try it sometime. I don't think it cures yeast infections though.

*I didn't get crabs the first time I had sex;
 I think it was the sixth time. I kid, I kid!

PART 5

Ain't That a Sham

Fakebook

Remember writing in a diary? We'd lock it, hide it, and eventually burn it to make sure nobody saw it or shared it with others. Now Facebook is the diary where we put our innermost thoughts and lose our minds if somebody *doesn't* see them and share them. *Why hasn't anybody noticed my post about eating an egg yolk this week? Don't they remember high cholesterol runs in my family!*

The best four years of my life were when I got off of Facebook (not to be confused with the years I *got off on* Facebook. Don't judge. That was when dick pics were still a novelty). The know-it-all posts, the awkward trying-to-be-sexy photos, the desperate self-promotion (and that's just my stuff). They should rename it Fuck-Face-Book because all of us on there are fuck-faces. I think we'd be institutionalized if we applied our behaviors on Facebook to real life. Imagine opening your door to find a stranger gleefully announcing to you, "Look at these delectable lemon squares I baked! I'm no Rachael Ray but, hello, I'm pretty darn close. Hashtag yummy. Hashtag there goes my waistline." Uh, hashtag new house, who dis? And why are you on my porch telling me this? Are my eyeballs supposed to turn into giant hearts as I wag my tongue at you?

What did people do before Facebook? Were they running into TJ Maxx on their anniversary shouting to anyone in earshot, "Attention everyone! This guy right here is the one who makes me count my lucky stars every day [*as they shove pictures of their wedding, a haunted hayride, and their firstborn's christening in people's faces*]. A man who lets me pick every vacation, every meal, and all the music on car rides? Yes, please! I'd marry you all over again, Mr. Best-Back-Rubber ever! Happy Anniversary honey! Hashtag pinch me."?

Pinch you? Maybe I should *punch* you because you were just complaining on the phone last week about how he's been plastered the last three years of your marriage and has gained thirty pounds since "joining the gym."

Facebook was once a place where people went to stay in touch with family and friends (AKA a cover to stalk their exes). Now Facebook is the Dress Barn of social media. It's outdated and embarrassing to patronize. The only people who go there on purpose are your aunt from Nebraska, guys with tits, people who peaked in high school, and Nigerian yahoo boys looking to tug at the heartstrings of many a passed-her-prime divorcée. Only on Facebook would a fifty-two-year-old woman who looks like Peter Griffin in a Dog the Bounty Hunter wig, with a temper like Gordon Ramsey, believe that a twenty-four-year-old, steely-eyed fitness trainer would want to travel across nations to get to her smoke-billowing pie hole and rusty vagina. Do these targets, I mean people, really believe these heartthrobs don't have access to any homegrown atrocious train wrecks? But I digress as that's more of a diatribe about *90 Day Fiancé* than Fakebook.

Messenger might be the worst thing ever to happen to humanity since man buns (really, cut it out . . . unless you look like David Beckham). I still don't even know the difference between "messenger" and "messages." People act like there's a sense of urgency if you miss their message, so they'll post on your timeline: "Hey, you didn't respond to my message. Are you pissed at me?" *I wasn't but 1) I am now even though I don't even know you, and 2) I just checked your message. No, that's not me in the random, suspicious video-link you wanted me to click on.*

I don't have Facebook on my phone and I only check it once in a while on my laptop. When I see a staggering number of messages, I panic. I don't know where to begin to respond, so I usually just run away instead and tell myself I'll deal with it next time. It doesn't mean I think I'm better than you. It just means I got distracted by a dust bunny floating by and that seemed like a more pressing matter to deal with at the time.

The worst is when people fight on your timeline—especially when it has nothing to do with your post! It's like being invited to dinner with a bunch of other couples and one couple starts having a domestic dispute at the table. Do you keep slurping your soup with your eyes down? Do you join in and start throwing dinner rolls? Do you try to break it up? I'm not a referee for crying out loud. I look horrible in vertical stripes.

And what's with all the work involved in posts? It's not enough to give a fake thumbs up anymore. "Don't bother liking this post if you're not going to copy and paste it to your page, tag sixty-seven friends, and leave a comment that starts with the first letter of your last name and the last letter of your first name. And sharing doesn't count!" Holy Jesus, take the wheel! Who has time for this stupidity? The messages are even worse: "Don't break this chain or bad luck will be heaped upon you for three weeks." Bad luck was heaped upon me when I accepted your friend request and started getting bombarded with your daily prayers, conspiracy theories, and zany "epic fails" video montages.

I get it. Your kid is the cutest, your gun is the toughest, your shrimp scampi is the tastiest, and this rant is the meanest. But would you be a dear and please like it, share it, repost it, copy and paste it, hang it on your fridge, and add it to your story? #Grateful

36

PRidE aNd PrejUDiCE and PARaDes

I enjoy being Italian (Italian American) but I'm not one of those extra loud, in-your-face, overly proud Italians. I don't have an Italian flag bumper sticker, I don't know anyone connected to the Mafia (. . . anymore), I don't make the sign of the cross every time my meatballs repeat on me, I don't flaunt my hairy chest (but that's only because I don't own an aggressively unbuttoned satin shirt and a cornicello necklace to prominently display), and I don't have my mom's face tattooed on my forearm and left ass cheek. I also didn't live at home until I was "finally ready to settle down" . . . at 75.

But so many people love declaring their pride over things they had no hand in achieving. I don't knock anybody for having pride in their accomplishments, or being proud of persevering after overcoming some crazy shit. That's not the pride I'm talking about. Being proud just because you or your ancestors were born somewhere? Adorning your vehicle with souvenir store crap to "represent" your pride? That's a little juvenile, isn't it? We all know those people. They wear muscle shirts in a blizzard to make sure you see their flag-blowing-in-the-wind tattoo on their chubby bicep. Why the tattoo? Are they afraid they're going to forget where they came from? How can they possibly forget something like that when they make it their entire identity? Then you have the people who are constantly crowbarring something about their ancestry into every conversation to remind you how "great" it is to be [insert nationality here]. *"You vill never 'ave a better meal my friend. Go ahead. Try. It's tofu dumplings vith varthog cheese."*

What I don't understand are the people who are so "proud" of their heritage that they want to fight about it. It just seems that the more pride these people have, the angrier they are when declaring it. If these people are so proud, why are they so pissed off? A few years ago, I was at a bar with some friends on St. Patrick's Day. I was standing there, minding my own business (AKA making bets with myself on which patron would spill their drink first while frenetically trying to dance to "The Impression That I Get" by the Mighty Mighty Bosstones) when all of a sudden, this short, stocky drunk with wild eyes in a backwards baseball cap starts screaming at me, "You don't belong here! This is St. Patrick's Day, not St. Guido's Day! Come on, take a shot. You know you want to." I just walked away. There was no way I was going to hit a drunk pregnant chick. Geez.

Whether it be national pride, religious pride, or body pride, people get wild about it. And with that pride comes prejudice towards those who aren't like them, and parades to clog up traffic. Who the hell enjoys a parade? They're the pits! Floats; marching bands; horrible attire; balloons the size of Will Smith's ego; music that sounds like a sad fart; the local news team waving to the crowd from a vintage Cadillac even though they all hate each other and the over-the-hill anchor with the toupée that looks like a permed squirrel doesn't even know where the fuck he is. I don't get the pageantry of such mishmash. What does any of that have to do with pride? It looks more like a precession of *Sábado Gigante meets Sesame Street* on steroids. Then the parade-goers plant their missionary-sex-only bodies in their flimsy Walgreen's lawn chairs to watch people walk by them. They plan their whole day around "getting there early" to find a spot to just see a bunch of strangers stroll by in a precession of b.o. I'd rather hang out at the DMV than one of these snoozefests.

And what happens if someone has multicultural and religious backgrounds? Maybe they're a Jewish Latina. What if the parades are on the same day? How do you choose which to attend and what to wear? You definitely don't want to accidentally show up to the Chasidic parade in your Latin parade ensemble. Tits and tzitzit definitely don't mix. And by the way, is there a parade-only-attire store that I don't know about that only sells things that are three sizes too small for people despite a significant Lycra to cotton ratio? Just because you have a belly doesn't mean you should wear a belly shirt (unless you want to be mistaken for one of the floats).

If people insist on having parades, at least make them tolerable. Get a real band to play. Turn the floats into ramps and have the classic cars Evel Knievel themselves over the crowd. Turn the giant balloons into piñatas filled with money, peanut butter cups and Epi-pens. And make the last float in the precession a streetsweeper to clean up the disgusting garbage left behind. A mess isn't something to be proud of, is it?

AmeRica's GOT TaleNt Show Sob StoriES

Way back in the day, talent shows were only about mocking people who sucked and letting d-list celebrities think their opinions mattered. Jaye P. Morgan didn't have to worry that the Unknown Comic would jump off a bridge if she gave him the gong. She and the rest of the talent show judges had a job to do, and it didn't include free psychotherapy to everyone seeking stardom in an attempt to fill a void left by a neglectful man-whore dad who was trying to fill his own void with a revolving door of wives.

The reason I hate the sob story routine so much is because it works. Now we have TV shows like *The Voice*, *America's Got Talent*, and *American Idol*. If they give me a cancer survivor, a trapeze artist who's just a torso, a large kid who was bullied in school, a survivor of a hate crime, a homeless vet, or a performer with a terminally ill parent, I'll collapse in a pile of tears before voting on my cell *and* my landline. I might even get a burner phone just to vote extra.

Maybe I'm an easy mark and get so emotional because *I* need to fill a void. I better talk to a psychotherapist. I wonder if Lionel Richie has any openings. *Hello* . . .

A DoNaTioN *in* YoUR NAme

There's a pretentious, shitty trend in gift-giving: the "donation in your name." Have you ever gotten one of these cheap pieces of crap? I'll never forget the first time I was hit in the face with this figurative turd wrapped in a bow. I got a birthday card from a friend with whom I always exchanged gifts. I got a card but no package, so I figured there had to be a gift certificate inside. But there wasn't. There was just a tiny piece of paper with the words *Happy Birthday! I made a donation in your name* typed on it. First of all, call me greedy, but if I can't eat it, wear it, put batteries in it, or regift it, I don't want it. It's not a gift to me. Secondly, my entire friendship with this person has been based on gifts. What the hell am I friends with you for if I have to listen to your whining all year without some sort of reward come birthday time?

The other problem with this sham disguised as altruism is, they never tell you what charity they donated to or how much they donated. If I don't know how much you spent on me, how am I supposed to know how much I like you? I certainly can't gauge our friendship on feelings. Not only that but if the donation was indeed made, how do I know you're not making me look like a cheapskate? When I donate, I do it anonymously, so I certainly don't want my name attached to something I had no say in choosing. What if it's some avant-garde charity I don't give a shit about, like Braces for Beavers? Don't get me wrong, I'm into charity. Juvenile Diabetes? Sign me up. Breast Cancer Awareness? I'm on board. Saving the Yellow-throated Cuckoo Bird? Shove it up your ass, you cheap, white, phony, esoteric, tree-hugging, sensible-shoe-wearing,

This-Is-Us-watching, swear-jar-enforcing, death-row-sympathizing, furniture repurposing, "my child was honor student of the month" bumper-sticker-having, hemp-poncho-wearing, arugula-eating, pescatarian douchebag.

And just a quick side note. Does anybody notice that the donation in your name people are also third-world country vacationers or *House Hunter International* clients? They think they're so cool with their Velcro sandals and fluency in Uzbek. They act like their kids are going to thank them for depriving them of American luxuries such as friends, nutrients, and morbid obesity rather than resent them for trying to be the hip, Tom's-toothpaste-using, *Eat, Pray, Love*-reading, handmade-gift-giving, shithead. But back to the original topic.

It's bad enough friends and family attempt to look like do-gooders supposedly donating on your behalf, or "instead of presents, how about we just donate to charity?" How about I already donate to charity and don't need accolades for it, but I do need awards for my superior gift-giving skills. And my gift-receiving skills aren't too shabby either so let me show those off too (unless you give me clothing in an animal print. Why do people who shop at Dillard's always assume that more stylish people love animal prints and clothes that sparkle? I'm not an eighty-six-year-old retired burlesque dancer). But it's even worse when grocery stores have huge boxes at the exits for customers to make food donations.

I'm sorry, what? This whole building is filled with food that can be directly donated. No middleman is necessary. Call me crazy, but can't the grocery store skip the extra step of getting others involved and just make the donation themselves directly from their own stash? Yet, they want us to buy the food, put it in a box that reads, "Please drop your canned goods here to help feed the hungry," and then let them take credit for it. "To date, the folks here at Stop and Plop have donated over nine kazillion-dollars-worth of food to help feed the hungry." Uh, no, you didn't. You sold food at a profit, we the customers bought it, and then dropped it in a donation box made from empty banana cartons (that could've been donated when they were still full).

Restaurants are hilarious when it comes to charity. Cheesecake Factory claimed to be "helping" feed the hungry with a Reese's Peanut Butter Chocolate Cake Cheesecake. Gosh, they are so generous for creating this over-indulgent, overpriced, diarrhea-inducing tower of sugar (that could feed a village) and sending a whole quarter from the sale of it to a place that doesn't even have running water. So, after gluttonously stuffing your misshapen, vacuum-like face with a frivolous seventy-nine-layer cake filled with chocolate, nuts, caramel, blood diamonds, and sweat-tears, you can feel so good about yourself knowing that, of the twelve dollars you spent to put you one bite closer to convulsing into a diabetic coma, twenty-five cents of it is going to charity.

"Hey Ethiopia, guess what we did for you? Rather than just sending you actual food, we created this outrageously humongous piece of cake that everybody but you can eat. Here's a roll of quarters. Don't spend it all in one place (like that grain of rice you've been eyeing or that divot in the road with the small collection of rain-water)." Here's a thought: How about sending the *actual cake* to feed the hungry? Better yet, how about opening a Cheesecake Factory in one of these countries? Can you imagine how long the wait would be?

39

The Kids ARE ALL White:

ANNoying White Kid Names

An annoying white kid name is typically born from the out-of-touch, condescending, no-rhythm body and brain of a J. Crew-loving white person. This breed of parents saddles their kids with pretentious names that make them sound like sixty-two-year-old bankers from the 1930s.

Boys should have names that don't sound like their only option in life is to be a trust fund recipient who kills call-girls who stay a tad too long at the frat party. Stick with the oldies but goodies like Nick, Rob, Steve, Chris, Mike, Scott, Matt; I'll even let an Alex or an Andy slide in (that's what she said). But for the love of God (which is also not a good name for your kid), please don't jump on the trendy name bandwagon. You'll end up with a self-absorbed asshole—and nobody needs more people like you running around.

Super-white parents think it's cool to give their kids ambiguous names that are a little bit coochie and a little bit bat and balls. Girls' names should be delicate and pretty like Ava, Sabrina, Lola, Gia (anything that ends in an *a* apparently), or stick with the basics like Emily, Katelyn, or Melissa that say, "I might bang you on the first date, but I wear turtlenecks to throw the public off." It's important to realize that certain names have predetermined traits. Have you ever met a non-douchey Chad or a classy Skyler? Does anyone know a Coleen who doesn't have a feathered perm? Ever come across a Jessie (male or female) who doesn't say *ain't*? How many girls named Destiny don't have a destiny to slide down a pole for a living? Have you ever been acquainted with a Regan (pronounced with a long *e*) who didn't smile with dead eyes?

And enough with taking Irish last names and making them first names. We get it. You're overly proud of your always-ready-to-fight-for-no-reason heritage. But is it absolutely imperative to shove a Brady O'Boyle or a McCauley McInerny down our throats? What's even harder to swallow (that's what she said) is when an Italian marries an Irish, and they try to "represent" both heritages, and you end up with a very tiny, very hot-headed Vito O'Herlihy who loves to expose himself at parades.

If you're reading this and getting offended, you *shouldn't* be reading this because you're an overly sensitive unstable weirdo with no sense of humor whose name is probably Ridge. But if you have balls of steel or tits of titanium, continue reading the list below of the most annoying white kid names on the planet:

Aidan, Braden, Brandon, Jayden, Colton, Reid, Reese (or Rhys), Chad, Cooper, Trevor, Cameron, Finch, Quinn, Bryce, Duncan, Finn, Haley, McKenzie, Chase, Case, Regan, Travis, Jackson, Connor, Tanner, Chip, Skip, Clay, Hunter, Wyatt, Cody, Ethan, Bailey, Noah, Morgan, Jacob, Parker, Peyton, Preston, Cortland, Everett, Addison, Riley, Mason, Emerson, Cole, Brady, Blair, Griffin, Jordan, Brody, Camden, Trenton, Clifton, Princeton, Atlantic City (just making sure you're still paying attention).

But my favorite, most nauseating white kid names come from a very special place: Megyn Kelly's Jokerish-looking plastic surgery head. The three most cringeworthy names bequeathed to children are Yates, Yardley, and Thatcher. Because you can't say these names without a locked jaw and clenched teeth is precisely what makes it difficult to take them seriously. Were they cut from a seersucker umbilical cord after exiting a Vineyard Vines vagina?

Keep in mind this is specifically about those trendy, overly white-sounding names. But many other names can make their own lists, like overused white girl names such as Whitney, Ashley, or Meghan. There could be a list of white trash/stripper names (Jasmine, Amber, Kim, Lexie, Crystal, Tiffany, Britney, Charity, Nikki, Star, Tami). The lists could go on with names containing unnecessary apostrophes or common names spelled irregularly in an attempt at being special: Kady, Leesa, Jayceson, Melanee, Jefri, Mykul, and Mishell.

Sorry if you're offended, but what other choice did I have than to get a sense of humor when given an uncommon name like Claudia?

40

Meatless Meat

Some things were meant to have meat, such as things with wings, things with ribs, and the vaginas of yesteryear. But for some reason, fast-food and white-trash chain restaurants want to bring in a new clientele: voluminous vegetarians. Hooters is now serving meatless chicken wings. And in keeping with the theme of giving customers things they don't want: all the waitresses will have A-cups and wear orange burkas. Along with several other restaurants, Burger King is also in the meatless meat arena serving the Impossible Whopper. What's impossible is believing it contains any actual food in the recipe. The first ingredient is water. The rest of the ingredients are a jambalaya of proteins made from soy and potato, followed by ingredients that end in *-ulose; -trose; -ine, -ide, and -nate.*

I have nothing against the idea of not eating meat. In fact, I wish I didn't love it so much because when I stop and think about it, it's horrifying and disgusting. But what I don't understand is this ruse of going to a fast-food joint for healthy options. A place that can give you "edible" meat in under five minutes—and shit-laced farts before your second bite—isn't qualified to provide healthy options. You're not going there to improve your life; you're going there because, until you can eat yourself into a recliner and get yourself an enabler, this is your comfort food. And purporting to be a healthy option when an Impossible Whopper contains fifty-five percent of your daily value of saturated fat is more ridiculous than Madonna's eye patch.

You don't go to Burger King to get your health on track; you go to clog your arteries and blame it on genetics. Just as you don't go to a strip club for the stimulating conversation, you go to see women diddling themselves for you while they yammer on about paying for nursing school. No guy has ever said, "Yeah, I'm not in the mood for tits today. I think I'll go chat with Destiny at Cooters about her financial woes and heavy course schedule."

What the heck is next? Monster truck jams with Smart cars?

SATURDAY! SATURDAY! SATURDAY! Get ready to be pummeled as Waffle House and Cabela's proudly present Truck-less Monster Jam! You'll see Sustainable Earth Shaker; Dainty Diablo; and everybody's favorite, Going Green Grave Digger! Only TWELVE BUCKS! TWELVE BUCKS! That gets you into the Fargodome, and two meal passes good for hemp hot dogs. See you SATURDAY! SATURDAY! SATURDAY!

It's getting out of hand with all these contradictory products. All I know is I'm not going to a drive-thru for healthy options, just as I'm not going to my mechanic for a colonoscopy... again.

41

The ROCK aNd ROLL HaLL of LamE

Many people have commented that it's not rock and roll to care about the Rock Hall. At first, it sounds cool to buy into that, but isn't it more rock-n-roll to say you don't care but then rage about it like a loose-lipped lunatic? Isn't the root of rock all about attitude and being pissed off? If there's anything a rocker loves most, it's fighting the man.

Every year, the Rock and Roll Hall of Fame announces its nominees, and every year, they reject the actual rock acts and get nobodies like me ranting and raving about the injustice—as if any of it truly matters. What matters here is that when it comes to complaining, I'm kind of a hall of famer. So let's get down to business.

For 2020, there were some rock nominees on the ballot, including Judas Priest, Pat Benatar, Thin Lizzy, and Motörhead. But instead, we got Biggie Smalls and Whitney Houston, we have a problem! I like a lot of Whitney's songs. I love her voice. I think she's a hall of fame singer. But I'm failing to connect Whitney with rock. But it's a little bit more palatable than a dude whose songs were really just other artist's songs with him rapping over them. "Big Poppa" samples "Between the Sheets" by the Isley Brothers. "Hypnotize" is really just Herb Alpert's "Rise." And do I need to remind you what gave "Mo Money, Mo Problems" its catchy sound? Ah, who the heck am I kidding trying to sound so aggravated? Some of those songs were pretty good, but not rock-n-roll.

I'm not suggesting any of this is important. Being inducted into the Rock and Roll Hall of Fame doesn't mean anything. It doesn't change a band's career or legacy. I'm just pointing out how it makes no sense. If anybody from any genre of music can be inducted, why not just change the name to the Music Hall of Fame? And if every type of music falls under the category of rock, then it must work in reverse. I can't wait to see Motörhead inducted into the Hip Hop Hall of Fame alongside Anne Murray and Flock of Seagulls. The Rock Hall is turning into the music version of the participation trophy. It doesn't matter if you were actually on the team, or even in the league, but here you go anyway! The eternal punk in me still says this is bollocks (my inner punk is British), but the older, lazy hypocritical me says, "When does the ceremony air? I need to stream it (so I can criticize it, of course)."

42

AA: ONE *A* at a Time

I'm not sure why I never understood the appeal of getting drunk or high. As a teenager, I didn't have that urge to "be cool," it just came naturally (as evidenced by my pining poetry and watching *The Golden Girls* every Saturday night with my mom). While everybody else was getting drunk and being popular, I was mentally preparing for the excitement of a potential Dick Van Dyke or Richard Mulligan cameo. *What kind of quagmire would Dorothy and the gals get into when one of these hunks showed up?*

Most of my friends are, and always have been, drinkers. Others also indulge in pot, some had their affairs with coke, and others may have experimented further. It doesn't bother me. As long as it doesn't affect a child or innocent bystanders, I don't care what you do. I have noticed that it seems like more people than not have some sort of drinking obsession. I say obsession because most drinkers have a problem with, well, the word *problem*. I realize I'm the weirdo for not relating to the excitement attached to excessive drinking. But I must admit, there's something odd about being invited to a nine-year-old's birthday party and realizing there aren't any other kids there. Poor Billy's kicking dirt while mom and dad play a flirtatious game of quarters with the neighbors. When the kid's party is really just a cover for all the adults to pound booze like their lives depend on it, maybe it's a problem. In their defense, though, how the hell else are you supposed to get through parenthood these days without anesthetizing yourself? Am I right, parents?

A few years ago, a friend asked me to go to his first AA meeting for moral support. He isn't one of those cute drunks who belts out "Party in the USA" while hugging everyone in the bar before disappearing—only to resurface the following day passed out on a stranger's porch in a fireman's hat. He's one of those emotional, sloppy drunks who screams out, "My parents never got me braces!" before setting fire to a stranger's porch and forgetting to pick his kid up from school . . . because he forgot he even had one.

I was excited to see the inner workings of one of these lifesaving meetings. I went in with an open mind and a slightly open blouse (hey, you never know where you're going to meet your dreamboat). Everybody was welcoming, kind, and seemingly unfamiliar with teeth-whitening products. We sat at one of many large tables that were pushed together into a u-shape so we could all see each other. One by one, people would introduce themselves as alcoholics. People shared different stories of how alcohol screwed up their lives. I wasn't sure how this was a deterrent. Most of the stories sounded so darn fun. It made *me* want to have a drinking problem. I sat there thinking, "Wait, you're telling me that if I have a few margaritas, I might inexplicably end up in an astronaut's uniform giving the Heimlich maneuver to an inflatable pelican in a stranger's pool? Sign me up!" But I had to mimic the others' reactions of empathetic disgust with a subdued head nod/head bow combo. A lot of the stories involved unseasonal nudity for some reason. I felt like I was at the "Only in Florida" news headquarters.

I liked that it was a comforting environment that didn't focus on blame. But the freewheeling no-fault policy seemed to encourage many folks at this meeting to imbibe, wreak havoc, and repent later. One gentleman even got up to discuss how he knows he'll slip the weekend his ex-wife remarries. The woman next to him gently stroked his forearm, telling him, "It's okay. We'll be here when you do. And a new set of chips will be waiting for you when that's behind you [*chuckle chuckle*]."

Another guy said, "I lost control and threw the remote at my wife." Well, did she change the channel during a playoff game? I mean, is booze really to blame, or is her continued poor judgment?

"I'll never forgive myself. I got drunk at happy hour and missed my son's recital." Isn't the thought of your son dancing in tights the reason why you started drinking in the first place? Is alcohol to blame, or your uptight, homophobic religious upbringing?

So, in summary: Go to AA if you want to get sober. Go to AA if you're not quite yet sober. Or just go to AA if you have a hankering for stale donuts, burnt Sanka, chips and story ideas for the next *Jackass* movie.

The Big Lie:

"Hello, My Name Is Toby. Thank You for Calling Customer Service"

I hate when I can't understand customer service people. It's even worse when they use American-sounding names as if that's somehow going to fool me into understanding them. Creating an uncomfortable situation from the get-go is the exact opposite of customer service.

Do they really think they're fooling anybody with this "Hello, my name is Toby" charade? People are already annoyed when they have to resort to calling customer service, so don't make it worse by forcing us to walk on eggshells for fear of being called racist when you give us a person we can't understand. Maybe customers should start rebelling and speak Klingon when they have to deal with this foolishness.

It's all well and good that everybody's getting an opportunity in the employment pool, but I think "Toby" would be better suited for psychic hotlines. Those companies would make a killing. Customers have to pay by the minute. If they can't understand what the psychic is saying, they must ask them to repeat it. People dumb enough to call will be dumb enough to stay on the line until they hear what they want regarding their shitty love life and horrible job. So swap out the English-speaking psychics with the fast-speaking foreign customer service reps. Will this work? My magic eight-ball says *signs point to yes*.

HaLLmaRK: WhEN YOU CaRE EnOugH To SeNd tHe VeRY BESt tO the VeRY Worst

Why hasn't Hallmark gotten the memo that lots of people suck? There's a lot of stress trying to pick out the right card, especially when the only choices paint a picture of roses and rainbows. Why don't they make cards for one-sided friendships? Why don't they make cards for parents who were just okay? You know, they just got the job done, but without any of the bells and whistles (like love and encouragement). Where are the cards that say *Thanks for putting "a goddamn roof over my head"*? We owe it to the people who suffered all their lives to get a few zingers in on those special occasions, so maybe I'll start a new line of greeting cards inspired by existing ones that I can put my own spin on.

Dad's birthday is always a reason to celebrate! Can't forget those dads who begrudgingly come home from work to the family they resent with every fiber of their being; the same family they can't afford but continue to expand because of their selfish refusal to use birth control. But hey, isn't that what shitty dads think kids are for; to take your frustrations out on?

This one's for you detached dads:

Dad, I just want to thank you . . .
   *for letting me stay when I was seven, even though
   I was "eating you out of house and home."*

You were always there . . .

   when it wasn't appropriate

     (I could grab my own bath towel).

You always listened . . .

   on the other end of my phone calls,

   when I talked to my girlfriends

     (The moaning was a bit much).

And I want to thank you . . .

   for not leaving any scars when you hit me

     (Not counting the emotional ones, of course, LOL).

The same warmth that was there for me when I was little
is there for me now . . .

   your heart is like a freezer-burned ten-year-old

   holiday fruitcake.

We're so close, I not only consider you my dad . . .

   but a raging hemorrhoid because you're always up my ass

   for every little thing

That's why I wanted to give you this card
to show you how much you mean to me . . .

   $2.75

     (before my 20% CVS coupon)

Happy Birthday!

   I hope it's your last!

HR

Everyone knows HR isn't your pal or protector. They're there to lure you with one hand held out while pushing you down the stairs with the other. When they disperse those "anonymous" surveys where you can "securely" vent your frustrations, and they assure you it's safe to report any issues without repercussions, they're really just trying to pluck you out like a pesky gray pube that keeps popping through your underwear.

HR isn't there to protect sick and tired employees from being the brunt of their boss's unpredictable mood swings. When your boss looks at you as if you took a crap on his credenza after he tells you, "Come on in anytime and let me know what's going on out there," it can make work a smidge uncomfortable. And we all know HR doesn't give a shit if other employees bully you because you're the only one who doesn't blow your load every time Linda brings in her peanut butter cookies. Anaphylactic shock or not, you're the outlier, and corporate is threatened by that.

It's the same response no matter what kind of company you work for—big or small. If you open your mouth, you're the problem. HR is there to protect the shitheads and weed out the people who aren't afraid to call them out. Unfortunately, I never met an HR employee with integrity, a sense of humor, or a candy dish with good candy (who the fuck still eats Jolly Ranchers and Fireballs?). It's a no-win situation, so you either have to suck it up, suck someone off, or wear seersucker and go work for Brooks Brothers.

SORRY CeLebriTiES

Have you ever noticed that whenever somebody's caught doing something terrible, they call their actions a mistake? "Honey, I'm sorry I stuck my dick in another woman. It was a mistake. It just fell in. I promise to be more careful next time." Accidentally buying nectarines when you thought they were peaches is a mistake. Ramming your penis into your coworker's mouth at happy hour isn't a mistake; it's Cinco de Mayo. Sometimes, cheating isn't a mistake; it's a condition. "Honey, my sex addiction has been acting up again. I had a gang bang with twelve Columbian Only Fans models and a boat captain last weekend. Dear God, when will there be a cure for this nightmare!" Calling it *sex addiction* rather than *cheating* allows the cad to keep "slipping up." It also allows the woman to justify staying with the cheater. If he has a "disease," it's not his fault, and she's a compassionate saint rather than a desperate loser.

Who even heard of sex addiction until [*probably*] a celebrity publicist had the brilliant idea to make us feel sorry for the cheater? After all, who doesn't sympathize with an afflicted individual? So now, when celebrities are called out after getting caught cheating, harassing, bullying, being racist, or just generally sucking, they issue a scripted apology that paints *them* as a victim by way of ignorance, illness, or being a model who thinks she has comedy chops. Stay in your lane Stilts!

I love how most celebrity apologies start with "I deeply regret . . . " even though, if they genuinely regretted it, they would've apologized before being outed. They often do a sorry-not-sorry type of amends in the style of Lea Michele ("I'm sorry *you* negatively *perceived* my words or actions"). And if they're caught harassing or bullying, they're going to go to rehab (even if they don't abuse substances) to get through *their* difficult time and learn why they behaved this way. They also assure the public they will spend their time "getting educated" and learning about the topic they "misspoke" on. Just how much does Chris Harrison need to know about antebellum balls before he can start hosting a dating show for damaged, delusional dimwits again?

In conclusion, I'd like to apologize if you were offended by anything I said in this book. I deeply regret that you bought it.

PART 6

Douchebags, Assholes, and Other Things That Stink

47

GeNdeR ReVeaL ZEAL

How much of a self-absorbed twat-face do you have to be to think anybody gives a shit about the gender of your unborn baby? It's either a boy, a girl, or still-undecided. And yet, these narcissistic gender-jerkoffs expect people to show up to a party and act bowled over when colored powder shoots out of a homemade M-80. "NO WAY!!! I can't believe it's a girl!!! I didn't expect this!! I'm so excited for you!!" It's either going to come out blue or pink (or beige for gender-neutral), yet these parents-to-be want people to react as if they just saw Prince come back to life from a homemade purple pipe bomb.

If you're not familiar with it, a gender reveal party is a celebration of someone ejaculating inside of you. Then you invite a bunch of family and friends to a gathering to reiterate that even morons can reproduce (as if the overly populated earth full of useless ass-wipes isn't enough of an indicator). The payoff is the aforementioned colored explosion. The guests are usually as stupid as the parents-to-be because they don't immediately call DCF to take the kid away as soon as it's born. If I were invited to see an explosion in a desert full of burnt-out shrubs (for some reason, these spectacles are always held in highly flammable locations), I'd have to wonder how fit these fucktards are to be parents.

We've seen plane crashes, broken bones, a death, and a 47,000-acre wildfire, yet these over-the-top announcements persist. The wildfire cost Arizona over eight million dollars! The dumb dad had to pay $100,00 plus $500 per month in perpetuity to repay the money it cost to put the fire out. And he thought diapers and formula would be expensive! I wonder how shitty the kid's life will be with parents who literally see money burning every time they look at her.

It seems that the dumber they are, the more elaborate the stunt has to be. With people so desperate to make an impression on social media, gender reveals are horrible trends that won't disappear. Interestingly, the mishaps and mayhem are the only things that make these look-at-me affairs worth their weight in gold. Or shall I say, worth their weight in pink or blue . . . or fire red?

48

Office BaRbs

Before venturing into comedy, I tried the office thing, but it wasn't for me because too many things annoy me . . . like people's faces. Especially the ones that look happy-stupid. It's not that they're ugly or mean; it's just that their face is happy and stupid at the same time. It's bad enough you have to spend your day with people who adorn their workspace with motivational quotes and Kennebunkport, Maine postcards, but these jobs expect you to remember all their ridiculous rules like show up on time; show up; don't maim your coworkers; wear underwear with your skirt (uh, okay, how am I supposed to get a raise? Duh).

According to American law, every office has to have a Nance, a Deb, or a Cath who loves green bean casserole and JC Penney blouses that include a pre-sewn-on tapestry vest. She's usually the chick from HR or accounting with the feathered perm and the really officey sounding name like Barb Jacobs or Connie Collins. You know who I'm talking about. She's the one who sneaks up on you in your cubical and speaks in that annoying, whispery voice and says stupid crap like, "Hey hun, working hard, or hardly working?" as she gives you a "supportive" shoulder squeeze. She's best known for her Pineapple Upside Down cake, mood swings, and using made-up words and phrases like "TGIF" or "I enjoyed sensitivity training."

And why is this busybody always soliciting money for the latest cause at her kids' school like Candles for Cancer or Ribbons for Restless Legs? Please! I can barely afford to fund my own cause: Liquor for Lunch to get through this horrible day (and I don't even drink). When she's not soliciting money for her kids' stuff, she puts on her birthday-bully hat and starts shaking you down for more money because now it's Dick Dozier's fiftieth. You don't know Dick, but there's a stupid card being passed around that you have to sign, and it always has some silly cartoon of the "whole gang" on the front and a really corny joke like, "A little birdy told us it was your 50th birthday! But we didn't believe it [open card] . . . because we only listen to talking emus!" Woohoo, what a hoot! There's a picture of an emu with a microphone and a cigarette. Dick is going to wish he turned fifty every day!

The only good thing about the office birthday is cake break. Barb coordinates everything, and if you don't own a pair of no-pocket powder blue elasticized-waist jeans, and you have a hairdo that debuted after the last season of Cagney and Lacey, she assumes you can't bake. So, in her signature whispery voice, she says, "Hey hun, could you be a doll and bring the paper goods?" And she always throws in a dig disguised as a joke like, "Oh, and no mini table-cloths! It's okay for your skirts, but the table is a bit more modest and prefers to cover its legs [insert fake adoring laughter]."

But even with all her quirks and passive-aggressive comments, we all love our office busybody. She's the reason we can look in the mirror every day and say, "I'm good enough. I'm smart enough. And doggone it, at least I'm not Barb."

49

DON'T WORK With the Public

If You Can't Keep

Your Shitty Attitude Private

Every time I go to my car mechanic, he says to me, "You're always smiling. You're always so happy." And I say, "Yeah, I always *pretend* to be happy." And then he comes out from behind the counter like a giant, cuddly predator on parole and says, "Give me a hug" as he "adjusts my headlights" and gives me a Gorilla Monsoon airplane ride (that's standard practice when getting your tires rotated, right?).

But back to "you're always so happy." I'm not always happy, but I don't blame the rest of the world for my inner turmoil (which is probably just trapped gas). I'm not rude or mean to people for no reason, and I don't walk around with a sourpuss (not that my privates are any of your business). Granted, most people make me want to cobra clutch them (two eighties WWE references in one rant. You're welcome!) within five minutes of meeting them, but I still try to be friendly, smile, and give them a chance. Apparently, this isn't the norm. What seems to be the norm is many adult crybabies who feel that their horrible life experiences justify treating strangers with disdain.

How is it that these masters of misery are always in jobs dealing with the public? Everywhere you go, there's an employee that makes you feel like you're bothering them at the job you're supposed to be bothering them at. Recently, I had to go to the hospital to pick up some records. The woman at the reception desk made eye contact with me and stared at me until I reached the counter. What happened next is mindboggling. She didn't smile or change her facial expression as I stood in front of her. She didn't greet me; she just continued to stare at me with a look of annoyed disgust on her face. Had she just eaten another box of Toaster Strudel? Was the yeast infection she contracted at the indoor waterpark acting up? Did she suddenly catch a glimpse of herself?

I don't like to make fun of people based on their looks, but once they act like an asshole, it's carte blanche. Of course, what accentuated her ugliness, even more, was her lugubrious demeanor. At first, I thought she was on the phone because she had a headset, so I didn't want to interrupt her. But when she continued to angrily glare at me, it wasn't until she rolled her eyes and let out an agitated sigh followed by "Uh, yeah, can I help you?" that I realized it was *my job* to greet the greeter.

"I'm sorry. I thought you were on the phone."

This time she grunted (or maybe she was clearing her throat after choking on a bit of self-hatred) before growling, "Whadaya need?"

When your face looks like a cross between a grouper, a Komodo dragon, and the product of inbreeding, shouldn't you be trying to detract from that with a pleasant demeanor and a friendly smile? A scuba diving helmet probably wouldn't hurt either. I guess I wouldn't smile either, though, if my teeth looked like paint swatches from the Sherwin-Williams Pee-Pee Poo-Poo collection.

Can you believe this is who was hired to greet people coming to visit their ill friends or family members? You walk in upset and worried, and now you have to be made to feel like you're imposing on the receptionist by expecting her to do her job—a job that involves looking up a name and providing a room number. She can't do this with a smile or without Fanta, a worn-out copy of *Fifty Shades of Grey*, and pictures of her Orange Tabbies strewn all over her workspace?

It's not just the receptionist at the hospital either. I've encountered this at doctors' offices, stores, and, most recently, a restaurant. I'm not sure if I can say the name, so I'll just call it Ruby "Thursday's." But they all have that attitude like, "Ugh, why are you bothering me?" Well, I'm bothering you, genius, because you're the idiot who signed up for this job—the job that includes working with the public. I'm sorry you had a shitty childhood, and your absentee father started another family with his new, younger wife, while your tear-soaked face was buried in your Teenage Mutant Ninja Turtles pillowcase every night. How about becoming a petty thief or an erratic yet lovable substance abuser like the rest of the troubled kids? Or how about becoming a goddamn great actress like me? Smile when you feel like crying, laugh when you feel like screaming, and always smile *and* laugh while you're repeatedly stabbing somebody. Remember, it's all about the polite presentation.

50

AbUSeRs, Racists, aNd HoMoPhobEs, Oh My!

A few things truly make somebody a bad person at their core: Hurting children and animals, committing hate crimes, putting ketchup on hot dogs, and being Jonathan Cheban fans. Abusers and racists are often one in the same and they always have shitty taste in music, insecurities that they think giant tires can quell, atrocious fashion sense (sheets with eye holes are never en vogue), and a level of "pride" far exceeding their IQ. But the abusers typically try to remain quiet and under the radar (until they explode at the Bubba Gump's waitress who forgot the extra tartar sauce) while the racists and homophobes are a little more freewheeling with sharing their "views." They put all their small dick energy into belligerently yelling when expressing their ideas. It reminds me of the cult leaders, political commentators, and televangelists whose messages are heavy on volume but light on substance or verifiable facts. *This white guy with blotchy red cheeks in a blue blazer and red tie with hair parted way too far on one side is saying things aggressively loud and needs to dab his sweat a lot; therefore, he must be an expert.*

Gay haters get infuriated over things that have zero power to harm them. How come they never have anger towards themselves for being sibling-fucking morons who hate the dentist, or for being gym rats with cartoonish Popeye muscles, or for being plastered-haired prep school dickwads that secretly want wads of dicks? Look how many varieties the homophobe comes in! They're interchangeable with racists and transgender haters. "Collect the full set and we'll give you a free Pastor Kenneth Copeland end-of-days-survival-kit!"

These guys are always unjustifiably confident and disgusted in their belief that every homosexual is going to hit on them. It never dawns on them that every *straight woman* isn't drooling over them and uninvitedly straddling them (and they're far less picky than any gay men I know). Still, they assume every homosexual is going to want their chafed-from-maniacal-masturbation peckers. And so what, even if they did get hit on? Now you know how uncomfortable women feel when we get attention from someone we're not interested in. But speaking for myself, I usually try to let them down gently. That's right. Gently. I can't think of a time a man I wasn't interested in hit on me and I flew into a rage that ended with me calling two of my closest friends to bring shovels and tarps "without any questions." My favorite argument that homophobes make is, "What's next? We're going to allow them to marry a llama?" Yeah, because that's a logical leap (except for the fact llamas can't write vows, give consent, or design runway couture, and everybody knows they prefer to spit, not swallow).

I saw a post from a woman on Twitter that said something to the effect of, " . . . just because I hate their lifestyle doesn't mean I hate them." The lifestyles of all the gay couples I'm friends with (two of them have been together for over thirty years) involve working, eating, watching TV, going to the beach, and a bunch of other mundane things that most people enjoy. My God, we must stop them immediately! Meanwhile, the hypocritical country cretin who posted that had to move her account from Instagram to Twitter because her husband found out she was having an affair with an over-fifty loser she met online whose handle was something similar to "UrGrownAssPoppa." People like her never get on a soapbox about child molesters, or seem upset with the lifestyles more native to hetero couples like controlling, nagging, having kids with anyone you sleep with, dragging your kids from relationship to relationship, buying furniture in sets, having a Lee Greenwood ringtone, or getting plastered in front of the kids.

Remember the Tampa Bay Rays players who wouldn't wear the Pride logo on their uniforms? They cited religious reasons. Aren't these the same guys who think prayers are meant to help grown men in tight pants hitting and catching balls? Is that in the old or new testament?

> *I want to thank God for helping us win today.*
> *I know he had to ignore all those prayers*
> *   for babies with brain tumors.*
> *With Him, anything frivolous is possible.*

First of all, what kind of animal doesn't love rainbows? Secondly, should stripper-licking substance-imbibers really be so pious over something so harmless and inconsequential to their lives? And stop with the argument about gays and trans people in the military. If somebody's willing to die for these un-United States of America, they deserve admiration, not a lesson on "values" from people who buy condiments in bulk and have kids out of wedlock because "marriage is just a piece of paper" (until a trans or gay person wants one of those pieces of paper).

Here's the bottom line: if you're worried about a person "marrying" a llama, you probably don't have much to offer the world anyway other than a bunch of recipes that all involve Campbell's soup and Cheez Whiz. You're gross.

Shopping Cart Shitheads

Is the urge to murder a normal reaction to seeing a suburban mom decked out in yoga attire cavalierly leaving her grocery cart in the middle of the parking lot? She spent $150 on exercise pants, but she's afraid to actually move in them? Or maybe she's just an entitled shithead who can't be bothered with common courtesy. Am I the only one who wants to run over the lazy slob who not only doesn't return his cart but even gives it a little push to send it careening through the parking lot? Not only do these monsters lack common courtesy, but it's a version of elitism: "Not my job. I don't get paid for that." These are the same losers who leave clothes in the dressing room, condescend waitstaff, don't say thank you when you hold the door for them, and idolize Ricky Schroder (Can't you picture him pushing a cart full of unpaid-for off-brand mayo and Brawny paper towels towards a Costco employee leaving work?).

Where do these beasts come from? I imagine it stems from parents who also have no manners. After all, they didn't have the courtesy to use birth control to prevent more assholes like this from being born. And *that* is the rudest gesture of all.

LicENse To PaReNt

Why is it that you need a license to fish, sell alcohol, sell real estate, breed dogs, or apply makeup to other people's faces, but any inept basket case can create life (ironically, most likely after drinking alcohol from a business licensed to sell it)?

Most people don't have the basic empathy or detective skills to be a caring but effective parent who won't release a future fuck-up into the world. When I hear a parent say their child is acting out, my antenna goes up, and red flags are raised. This is when you need patience, tenderness, and compassion because, most of the time, something is going on, and they don't know how to articulate it. Instead, what do most lazy, selfish parents with an authoritarian complex do? *I told her if she doesn't straighten out, she's off the soccer team, and she's not watching any TV for a month!* Wow, way to go! They took away the one thing that's probably a positive in her life and punished her for being upset or tormented by something rather than get to the bottom of it and help her through it. Oh, and in two years, when it comes out that she was being bullied, or worse yet, molested by mom or dad's latest fuck/stepparent of the week, they'll send *her* to therapy instead of themselves.

Kids and teens often act out due to a parent's horrible behavior or the unsettling, chaotic chore of having to go back and forth between parents' homes. The parents are the ones who should have to leave the house from week to week while the child stays in one place. The parents fucked up, yet the kid has to deal with the instability of no permanent home and "visiting" a parent (probably with their new family, thus making the child feel like an outsider).

Instead of the parents getting treatment to fix themselves and review the pitiful choices that led them to have a child they're not equipped to nurture, they make the kid think something's wrong with them and therefore are the ones that need to go to therapy.

If a grown man comes home from work and starts acting moody and unpleasant towards his partner, maybe they should take away his phone, his TV privileges, or anything else that brings him joy, just to teach him a lesson. *No Coors Light and cuckhold porn for you tonight, mister!* Oh, and for all the parents who think that hitting and humiliating kids are a rational solution when they irritate you or attempt to talk back, your boss and coworkers should beat you anytime you irritate them. It seems reasonable, doesn't it? "What do you mean the TPS report isn't done yet? [*Smack! Pow! Bam!*]" And showing up late for work, even just two minutes, warrants a week of cleaning your coworkers tinkle off the bathroom floors, walls, toilet seats, those damn aforementioned TPS reports, and wherever the hell else employees haphazardly urinate because it's not their own bathroom.

And let's cut the shit with being the grades Gestapo. Not all brains and talents are created equal. Not everyone is an A student. Not everyone can be on the honor roll, just as not everyone can be the best singer, the best athlete, or the best scientist no matter how much they study, or practice. Stop bullying kids into grades they're not capable of achieving. It's one thing if you know your kid is slacking off, and he can do better. But for chrissakes, stop punishing kids for reaching their potential. Most people are just average (commonplace, typical, ordinary, regular), and lots are below average. Look at you. You're the idiot who had a kid you didn't want. And if you're a parent who's being criticized for disturbing behavior, don't tell me I can't comment because I've never been a parent. I may not be a parent, but I've been a child. Do I also need to be a rapist or serial killer to have an opinion on their monstrous behavior? I'm not saying parenting is easy. In fact, that's why I believe a lot more thought needs to be involved in making that decision. And as evidenced by the state of this country, it's apparent poor parenting decisions have been going on far too long, resulting in all the lost, angry, gullible, triggered, wackos littering this earth . . . that some believe is flat (thanks crappy parents for those winners). And coddling your kid, never telling them no, and never holding them accountable for anything is just as neglectful and damaging as the rest of the shitty "parents."

Maybe you're reading this thinking the government is already too involved in our lives. I beg to differ. If we could find enough lawmakers with some balls, we'd have a law in place that imposes sterilization on anybody who's proven they suck at life. Let's put the Soup Nazi in charge. Imagine if he was promoted to Shitty Parent Nazi? Can't afford to move out of your parents' house? *No kids for you!* Your natural stench is mildew and smoke? *No kids for you!* Substance abuser? *No kids for you!* You've ever defensively referred to yourself as a "grown-ass" man or woman? *No kids for you!* Your toenails have injured another person? *No kids for you!* You'd disown your kid if they were gay or trans but stand by them if convicted of rape, murder, or molestation? *No kids for you!* You have carpeting in your bathroom? *No kids for you!* Your go-to talent at bars, PTA meetings, and family holidays is tying cherry stems with your tongue? *No kids for you!* You think dry-humping is dancing? *No kids for you!* But please stick to that instead of actual fucking.

CONCERT CURMUDGEONS

Anybody who goes to a concert and expects people to remain seated like a bunch of sedated nursing home zombies should be trampled. Obviously, I do not include people who physically can't stand. I'm referring to the outraged psychos who scream at everyone around them to sit down. Musicians feed off of the crowd's energy. If you don't have any, that's fine (maybe some of that "SIT DOWN!!" energy can be put into clapping . . . or walking . . . to your car... buh bye). With my health condition, I never know if or when I'll have energy. If I'm lucky enough to be at a show but can't get up, I'm certainly not going to ruin the guy's good time in front of me by demanding he sit down. It's not his fault I have shitty DNA.

When Steven Tyler runs around the stage for two hours straight, do you really think he wants to stare into a sea of mopey shitheads politely planted in their chairs with absolutely zero urge to move to "Sweet Emotion"? No musical performer on the planet is thinking, "Thank God for that riled up guy in cutoff jeans and black socks whipping the crowd into shape. I'm so glad he's berating everybody into sitting down and behaving like they're at a sixth-grade dance recital . . . or a Josh Groban concert." Concerts are for three things: Dancing, dressing slutty, and slutty dancing. The only person who will tell me to sit down is Nikki Sixx! And hopefully, he means on his lap.

The O.G. (ORiginal GROPER): CoSbY, COSBy, PuddiN' PiE. KiSSed THe GirLs, DruggEd Them, and MadE THeM Cry

Poor Bill Cosby. He lost steam as the most prolific predator in Hollywood. But let's not forget that he's a horny hypocrite and just as awful as the latest crop of pigs on parade. Who knew that when he preached to young black men to "Pull up your pants!" he really meant *before she comes-to*? We thought he was just giving some fatherly yet condescending fashion advice. And who knows fashion better than a man who became more famous for his busy, shapeless, seizure-inducing sweaters than for his comedy?

I was never on the Bill Cosby bandwagon. I wasn't drinking the Kool-Aid (or eating the drug-laced Jell-O) like most of America. Sure, I liked *Fat Albert* and his gang of neighborhood goofballs, but the actual Bill Cosby, not so much. Something about him always rubbed me the wrong way (and I wasn't even unconscious). Maybe it was how he looked down on others (especially when they were passed out beneath him), or his constant preaching of family values (while he was secretly fathering an illegitimate child with another woman), or his unfunny, overrated comedy (which would be enough to put anybody to sleep). Instead of spending money on Roofies and Quaaludes, he could've just forced them to listen to one of his bits. I just never cared for the guy.

It's scary that people still defend him. They act like his actions don't count as rape because he wasn't lurking outside a window in a ski mask with duct tape and rope.

"Nope, can't be a rapist. He had on a teal, diarrhea-and tinkle-colored patchwork robe with a cartoonish-looking paddy cap. The only thing he's guilty of is sporting some sassy PJs!"

Oh, and he's famous for pretending to be an educated, non-rapist, well-to-do family man on TV, so the allegations can't be true. Whoopi Goldberg was a big defender, often singing Cosby's praises. I wonder if she also thought this wasn't *rape-rape* as she stated about child sodomizer Roman Polanski. Maybe when you're a poor, unknown guy violating women, you're a rape-rape rapist (or would it be a rapist-rapist?), but if you have money and fame, you can only be two things: innocent and a target of some big conspiracy. Yeah, because all famous people are law-abiding, morally sound (Woody Allen; R. Kelly), well-behaved folks (Mel Gibson) who can do no wrong because money and popularity can cure inherent psychological defects. Only poor, talentless people can commit crimes because they can't direct movies and sell-out concerts. But because he's famous, he's not looked at as the monster he is. It's looked at as a bit of idiosyncrasy in his personality. "Aww, he's just eccentric."

Then there are the people who feel sorry for his wife. "Poor Camille." Really? You don't think this zip-lipped, subservient, blank-staring robot knew what her hero hubby was up to? Maybe not initially, but she certainly did after the deposition where he admitted to drugging women with Quaaludes. I wonder how she stayed with him after discovering that he had an affair that produced another child. But okay, sometimes people try to work it out after cheating. But who stays with a calculating, googly-eyed, popsicle-peddling, mush-mouthed, perverted pretend family man with a pretend Ph.D. who violates women? He wasn't even going out and hunting these women down. He was orchestrating scenarios where his victims were brought to him. He was the conductor of the sexual assault symphony. So, how did Camille look him in the eye? No, seriously, how did she look at those filmy eyeballs that look like ping pong balls dipped in cigarette ashes?

He was allowed to live a joyful, opulent life for years without any punishment for his crimes because Americans like to turn a blind eye (and apparently now he can too since he's blind as a bat, or as blind as a rape victim temporarily knocked out by a spiked drink) to famous goody-goodies. Even if their entire persona is a lie, Americans ignore the reality in favor of what they want to believe to suit their own comfort. We've had to suffer for years with his horrible stand-up, mumbling commercials, and his proselytizing about saggy jeans. Finally, America's Dad got put in timeout with other sexual predators who might not be so picky about their prey. He better hope a burly dude named Tiny doesn't ask for a lick of his famous Pudding Pop.

———

July 2021 Update: His conviction was overturned. In the words of AC/DC: "Lock up your daughters, lock up your wife, lock up your back door, and run for your life."

55

Mama June

If little boys are made of snips, snails, and puppy dog tails, and little girls are made of sugar, spice, and everything nice, is Mama June made of selfish choices, receding gums, and cookie crumbs? She had weight loss surgery, so WE tv gave her a show, and now she's in the news every other day. Every time I see a story about her, I pray she'll go away (Hey, if people can pray for things as frivolous as a football game, why can't I pray to unclog America's toilet?). The fact that this mush mouth, pedophile-loving, illiterate, human Big Mac can reproduce proves that God has a peculiar sense of humor and that apparently, you *can* defecate from your birth canal. Yes, I'm saying I'd like to hop in a time machine, thwart the conception of June, and stop the cycle of future disability-collecting, scooter-riding, Spam-eating, pedophile canoodling morons who are over-populating this country and subjecting children to their damaging ways. I feel bad for her kids, including Honey Boo Boo. Sadly, she's being raised by someone who puts men, crack, food, and fame before her children.

Who looks like a deformed, less appealing Bruce Vilanch and thinks, "I should eject babies from my cooter like a Pez dispenser and force them into the beauty pageant circuit"? And no matter what a child looks like, putting her in a beauty pageant is disgusting and irresponsible (unless her Marilyn Monroe impression is uncomfortably seductive. Then it's just a waste not to share that with the world. Yikes!).

June's first show, *Here Comes Honey Boo Boo*, was dropped by TLC when it came out that June was dating Mark McDaniel—the molester of her daughter, Anna Cardwell. After serving time for the crime, she welcomed him back with open arms (but that's only because she can't actually close them).

"Aww, he's rehabilitated. He did his time. It doesn't matter that my daughter is scarred for life. He deserves another chance because I'm a mangled amoeba in stretch pants who will serve my kids up on a silver platter [*or in her case, a Styrofoam plate*] just to get attention from a man. I don't care if it's just a ruse to get to my babies that I claim are priority number one in my life." Author's note: Whenever somebody says, "they did their time" or "he didn't actually touch anyone" regarding a pedophile or molester, I want to strangle them. Even if their crimes were "only" online (watching child pornography), they are getting off on and **contributing** to, the disturbing violence perpetrated against these helpless victims whose lives are ruined. So fuck off!

So, WE tv decided the world can't live without this maternally vacant procreator and gave her a show called *From Not to Hot*. Really? We're so politically correct that we can't even call a pedophile-protector gross? We're worried about hurting her feelings? Worse yet, do we have to pretend she's hot just because she dropped a few pounds? I don't think she's so much hot as she is sweaty. Her eyes always seem half-shut (unlike her corn dog shoot), and before her makeover, her teeth looked like a ramshackle staircase stuck to a wad of gum. Now she smiles, and it looks like a refurbished staircase painted in Wite-Out . . . stuck to a wad of gum.

Maybe if June had focused on her kids instead of pedophiles and crack, she wouldn't look like a haggard, smoky grandmother whose only exercise is thumbing through a Finger Hut catalog while farting out the remains of her Shake-N-Bake feast. I recall catching a few episodes of *Here Comes Honey Boo Boo* back in the day. I mean, they needed subtitles for people to understand them ... IN THEIR COUNTRY OF ORIGIN! A drunken Ozzy Osbourne would be easier to understand than these garbled hillbillies. What's ironic about the subtitles is that most of the people watching probably can't read them anyway.

56

FooTPRiNts in the

Sand-COLoReD CaRPEt

I hate being invited to a party and being told to take off my shoes. Actually, I just hate being invited to parties. You know what's grosser than dirty shoes entering your home? Feet! You've got your bunions, calluses, corns, fungus, hammertoes, extralong toes that don't match the other toes, that crooked toe that rests on top of the other toe, flat feet, fat feet, brick feet, feet that could've been walking around barefoot outside or on their own filthy floor before coming here, and feet that some secret perv at the party is going to be mentally cataloging for his fetish fantasy later. What about somebody who may be missing a digit or two? "Sorry Frank. We didn't know you had your big toe amputated." (Oops, now everybody knows Frank's a diabetic with no self-control who'd rather have a toe chopped off than give up Mountain Dew—but at least their floors are clean).

If I'm invited to one more gathering and told to remove my shoes upon arrival, I'm going to have taps permanently installed on my feet so I can prance all over your floors like a toddler being bullied by *Dance Moms'* Flabby Lee Miller.

"Remove my shoes? No prob . . . five, six, seven, eight *[tap, tap, tap, tap, tap, tap]* . . . this way to the kitchen?"

Have you ever noticed that the people who have this rule never tell you in advance? So, not only do I feel exposed and scrutinized (sounds like a Harvey Weinstein documentary), but now I have to be subjected to other people's feet who were also blindsided by this demand. I'm not interested in getting familiar with somebody's hygiene at a "congratulations on your promotion" party as they unveil talons that look like a tray of Fritos Scoops.

When I'm invited to a party, I try to show respect by dressing up (depending on the occasion). Most of my dress pants are too long (because the rest of me is too short), so I wear heels to keep the hem from dragging on the floor. It's inconsiderate to expect me to ruin my pants—and ultimately look like a slob—just because you don't want to mop, are afraid of scratches, and believe you're going to get sick from floor germs. Unless you're licking the floor or licking your fingers after caressing the floor (why the hell are you seducing the floor?), how are you catching anything from peoples' shoe remnants? I'm a frequent tinkler, and you want me to walk barefoot into your bathroom and risk stepping in something left behind by another partygoer who had bad aim (or bad pigs in a blanket followed by liquid diarrhea that expelled like a spray tan)? And if I did step in something, now I'm traipsing it through your house for others to spread around. At least shoes would act as a foot condom. I'd rather have a stinky shoe than Hep-B toes.

I also don't want to get to your house and watch other unsuspecting guests awkwardly struggle to remove footwear. People are holding each other for balance and putting legs in positions they don't belong. There's always an unwanted panty shot you can't unsee, and somebody always ends up piling their smelly Jesus sandals right on top of the brand-new shoes you bought specifically for this party that suddenly feels like a preamble to a cult suicide pact. The only place you see large groups of shoeless white people is in a documentary about brainwashed religious devotees, or fat naked swingers (sidenote: why do swingers always have weird bodies and hair in all the wrong places?).

Feet are ugly, so we should cover them whenever possible. Bare feet are for the beach, the bed, and the shower. Bare feet don't go with *any* outfit. Who puts on a pair of khaki cords (no, really . . . who wears khaki cords outside of 1987?) and says, "You know what would look great with these slacks? My forest green fleece Eddie Bauer vest and a callus-ridden hammertoe."?

Have you ever been subjected to one of these affairs? Doesn't it feel so bizarre when you're standing in a kitchen amongst a group of frumpy, shoeless white people eating Swedish meatballs on toothpicks and sipping Merlot while talking about their escalating oil bills and what a "hoot" their cat Tony is when he watches *Big Bang Theory* with "mommy and daddy"? And for some reason, they think lawn care is a "hot-button" topic ("that branch missed Lloyd's mower by *thismuch*"). All you can think is, *Whoa, slow down there. Bare feet and stimulating conversation? Did somebody open the gates to heaven because that's where I must be right now!*

When you invite guests to your home, their comfort should be paramount to your own. If you're a shoe oppressor, what's the most fun we could possibly have at your house anyway? Let me guess: a zany game of pious Pictionary? A walk down memory lane recounting the lovable quirks of late, stubborn aunt Stella?

Life is meant to be lived, rules to be broken, shoes to be worn, floors to be walked on, and uptight people are meant to be shaken, not stirred.

57

Joke Thieves

I'll never forget my early years in comedy. When you're starting out, chances are the only place to try out your jokes are open mics or contests. I crafted a bit about public breastfeeding (it happened to be a hot topic at the time), and I used it for my online audition into a radio-sponsored comedy contest. Each contestant had a video on the local radio station's website that people could vote for. The top five or ten (I don't remember the number) made it to the contest and got to compete live at the local comedy club.

Since people already saw my breastfeeding bit online, I figured I'd perform different material live. I knew most of the competitors, including a guy I'll call Archie, Conan, Ginger, or David Caruso (are you picking up what I'm putting down?). We chatted before the contest began, I wished him luck, and when he hit the stage, I couldn't believe my ears. He was doing my breastfeeding bit, almost verbatim! I thought maybe I imagined it, but when other comics and people in the audience who came to see me commented after the show, "Isn't that your joke," I knew I wasn't losing my mind. I didn't confront him ("Hey! That's my tit-suckling bit!") because I don't like to be the one to initiate confrontation (but when pushed, I'm good at finishing one). So, I just avoided the guy after that. He also stole a job opportunity from me some years later. I won't bore you with that one, but in a nutshell, he stole an envelope with my audition tape off the front desk—twice—so it would never make it to the radio station's GM. That was a blessing, though, because I think I would die if I were relegated to an "entertainment" career in western Massachusetts.

A few years back, a major headliner stole from me on the weekend we worked together. Once he heard my bit, he used it as his own every show we did together that weekend (and probably since). There's a comic known for being a joke thief in a certain region of the east coast. I wasn't aware of it when I first met him at a club one night. A group of us were having a conversation, talking about comedy, life, etc. Someone made a joke, and I retorted with a joke of my own. The joke thief commented how funny it was. I told him I use it once in a while on stage. Twenty minutes later, he's on stage doing my joke—and it killed. He also performed a bunch of jokes he stole from some Comedy Central roasts.

I've heard people ask what the big deal is if somebody takes your jokes. I can't even believe it needs explaining. Whether it's a joke you came up with on the spot during a show or one you've worked on for a while, it's an idea that came out of your head from your innermost thoughts to share with strangers. When somebody performs it as if it's their own, that's a punch-in-the-gut moment. I think anyone in any line of work would be livid if somebody else got credit for their work. I can't imagine anyone would be okay with Justin Timberlake hijacking writing credit for "Hey Jude." Stealing intellectual property is the lowest of the low. It's lazy. It's slimy. But worse than lifting a joke is stealing material, taking credit for it, and making a concerted effort to portray the rightful author as stealing it from you!

I was about twelve years into comedy when I met Robin Staint. She was brand new to comedy. The booker on a show I was working on gave her a spot as well. I always try to be friendly with everybody because I know what it's like to feel left out. I go out of my way to include people. I'm like this no matter the environment, but I'm even more cognizant of it with new comics because I imagine the nerves and uneasiness they must be feeling. I try to put people at ease with a welcoming conversation and words of encouragement. After speaking with Robin, I offered to recommend her to a club I'd been working for years. True to my word, I got her a guest spot (an audition). Unfortunately, she bombed. Fast forward a few years, and I'm working a gig that Robin Staint attended as an audience member. She's sitting at the table with the comics, and for reasons unknown to me, she's lukewarm to me. It's not my fault her super original "it's so hard dating as a chick" material didn't win the crowd at her audition. Or maybe the chill was because she was with her boyfriend and my killer-set night, and her body-by-cake night was making her feel threatened (I should note, I don't make fun of people's looks unless they try to hurt me or someone I care about. Act ugly? Expect to be looked at as ugly). I always open my set with some crowd work to warm up the audience. I have a couple of staples that I've used for years (including the years before Robin ever stepped her unfeminine hooves into the comedy arena) and some stuff I do on the spot.

A day or two after the show, she posts something on Facebook. It's a passive-aggressive post directed at me. She includes a bunch of pictures from the show and says something to the effect of, "Comedy 101: Always open with a bit about [insert my joke here]." At first, I thought it was an attempt at a compliment until I read further. She and a friend commented back and forth with sarcastic remarks mentioning how Robin always kills with this bit (implying I stole it). WTFuck-off! But I realized what happened. She stole it from me, but her boyfriend saw me doing it that night after seeing her do it on a previous occasion. She must've been so embarrassed (hard to believe this was more embarrassing to her than the first time he saw her polish off a Blooming Onion like an apple), so she had to save face before the truth came to light. So rather than acknowl-edge it, I did what any mature adult would do. I created my own passive-aggressive post. I even offered her a gig since then just to prove that she is terrified to face me, and sure enough, she declined the offer after taking a few days to even respond. That must've been a lot of diarrhea to handle those few days.

People ask why I don't confront these people. The answer is because it's fruitless (her body is also fruitless . . . it's mostly deep-fried). They'll maintain it's just a coincidence or parallel thinking. I'm not sure how she looks at herself in the mirror or how she sleeps at night (but I imagine it's with a CPAP mask and several empty Ben & Jerry's containers).

Public Maskurbation

I'm kind of sad that mask-wearing is declining. There was something comforting in not having to see other people's uncooperative, uncomely faces. I happen to love masks. I hate wearing makeup and I don't do Botox, fillers, or plastic surgery, and I can't keep up with all of my chin whiskers at this point, so I'd much rather put on a mask. I wish a respected leader—like LeBron James, Jennifer Aniston, or Batman—could mandate masks as well as sunglasses so I could hide my eyes too. I've had to roll them more than ever since 2020.

And why is it always fugly, nasty-toothed, bad breath stinkpots with the most obnoxious personalities who feel they don't need a mask when they're the ones who need permanent ones? My motto for those people is "No Mask? Wear a Casque!" They won't know what a casque is, or bother to look it up (but will declare they're an expert on them like all other things they espouse about). Actually, muzzles would be an even better choice. We don't need to see their fifty shades of grey teeth and hear their frenetic hyperbole, chip-on-the-shoulder reactions to minor inconveniences and hare-brained reasons why they "won't kowtow to the overlords!" and the declaration, "I have a medical reason for not wearing a mask!" Uh, no you don't. Feeling threatened and triggered by someone telling you what to do isn't a medical condition; it's a personality disorder. And don't get me started on religious exemptions (not just concerning masks). If they don't want to wear one, they shouldn't go to places that have every right to require them. Somehow, common courtesy and common sense (or lack thereof) has become politicized. And being vaxxed isn't an excuse to forego a mask. There are some rare instances where people can't get vaccinated. My friend's daughter can't get vaxxed because of a clotting disorder. One of my specialists recommended I don't get vaccinated due to the complexity of my medical conditions. Since he's the hottest of all my doctors, and the only one who listened to me (thus diagnosing my rare neuroendocrine cancer), I value his opinion the most. I don't run around to businesses or events that require people to be vaccinated and hold misspelled signs while screaming into a bullhorn that I'm somehow being discriminated against. I just don't go. And when I'm forced to be in public for medical appointments, I slap on a mask. I don't have a hissy fit and purposely wear it under my nose, on my head, or make a mask out of a thong like I saw some lard-ass do at one of my appointments. He even wore it inside out. He probably should've washed it. We didn't need to know that his mom had untreated vaginitis.

I love the people screaming at school board meetings, "UNMASK OUR KIDS! WE NEED TO SEE THEIR SMIIIIIILES!" Fuck off! They're already not smiling living with a loudmouth bully of a parent. Let the poor kids be masked so they can mutter their murderous musings when their preposterous parents embarrass them for the umpteenth time. When there are so many things to be justifiably enraged about such as Elaine Bredehoft's voice, Dairy Queens that are only open seasonally, Ted Cruz's hair, and Just Mayo being discontinued, doesn't it tell you all you need to know about a person when wearing a mask is the thing they choose to be intrusively vocal about? I can't imagine *that* being the sword I fall on—albeit a Nerf sword. It's also ironic that most of these complainers are the same people who call younger generations "snowflakes," yet they can't handle the thought of themselves or their kids being minorly inconvenienced by following a temporary rule. Doesn't a little adversity and structure build character and actually prevent kids from turning into snowflakes? Coddling your kid and making them think they're above the rules of common decency seems to be more of a catalyst for turning your kid into a nonfunctional, pill-popping, anxiety-riddled young adult, than teaching them that life is not all about them. Refusing to do something simply because somebody told you to is a little eighth grade, isn't it? Isn't that the age when you test boundaries and rebel against authority? At thirty-seven, shouldn't you kind of grasp that certain "rules" have a purpose other than setting you off like a roman candle?

And what's with people not grasping the concept of barriers? You have screens to keep out critters; pan lids to contain liquids; condoms to avoid cold sores, blisters, bleeding, discharge, and pregnancy; and goggles to protect your eyes in case your meth lab explodes. When I brought my friend to chemo treatments for four years (long before Covid), I never once felt infringed upon or violated by the sign requiring visitors to wear masks to protect others. I didn't scream at the employee at the front desk about "muh rights and muh freedoms," and I never sent messages to family, friends, or someone I follow on social media to bemoan the imposing nerve of having to have consideration for others outside of myself. I never dated a man who flew into a rage when required to wear a jacket at an upscale restaurant. I never claimed my civil rights were being violated because I couldn't wear a thong—and nothing else—to church and twerk my way up to receive communion (Note to self: join Lizzo's church).

The trait I've noticed about these people is they feel inferior to others for various reasons (intellectually, physically, financially, personally, etc.). Thus, they believe by being part of a fringe group, they're asserting their superiority for "figuring out" something you can't grasp. That evolves into believing their civil liberties are being violated, and somehow, society can be controlled by dint of a face covering. When pressed for specifics, they can never explain why the government would choose to "control" them by containing their droplets with a piece of cloth versus controlling them by removing their reproductive organs and sewing their mouths shut. Nor can they provide examples of how they'd be "controlled" beyond wearing the mask. There's no endgame that they can point to or explain, yet they're convinced that the non-peer-reviewed memes they giggle over are of substantial evidentiary value. If a Maskhole has a hepatitis-C-positive Waffle House server gushing blood from a cut on his hand and refuses to wear a bandage, or drools like an overheated Saint Bernard, they will suddenly have a ragefully revised meaning of their "God given rights!" And when one of these quacks needs heart surgery (trust me, they will), I'm sure [wink, wink] they're cool with the surgeon skipping a mask or not sanitizing their tools because it's the doc's goddamn American right not to wear "a co2 trap!"

I have nothing against stupid people. My issue is with arrogantly confident, perpetually enraged, stupid people. The level of confidence is so incongruous to the level of emotional intelligence that it almost makes sense—because you'd really have to be that stupid to be that confident. It's kind of like the sloppy-bodied chicks who wear everything three sizes too small and declare how they're the "sexiest bitch" ever.

Here's the deal. Isn't it fair to say most, if not all of us, don't want to be ill (Munchausen fans excluded, of course)? And if we have family or friends that we care about, we probably don't want them to be ill either (Munchausen by proxy fans excluded, of course). So stop behaving as if you're being asked to wear a mask for the rest of your life rather than to potentially help save a few for a temporary amount of time (which would go by a lot quicker if some people actually got the concept). And even if *you* don't believe in masks, why can't you suck it up the way I suck it up when I'm with a religious person who wants to pray in my presence? It's not harming me, so I respect their right to do what makes them feel safe. And when I'm at church for a wedding or christening, I dress frumpy and try to stifle my burps until the music gets loud.

I saw a tweet that somebody posted asking (in a mocking way) why somebody would be wearing a mask alone in a car. The bigger question is, why would they care? While they were being antagonistic, I realized they were that stupid to not be able to think of possibilities, so here's a list:

- They left one store and are heading to another that requires a mask
- Fillers gone wrong. Better to wear a mask than look like you have two Vienna sausages for lips
- They went down on a stripper at the early bird buffet. They need to get past the wife when they walk in the door.

Anyone who mocks masked people who are minding their own business probably still thinks De Niro impressions are the height of comedy. We're supposed to value that guy's opinion over reality? So, please shut your shit-shoot if you've never read the Harvard Medical Journal or a few studies from the Cleveland Clinic—on any topic; not just Covid. And how is a guy with the gall to wear jorts afraid of how he'd look wearing a mask?

The Shorts All-Year-Long Guy

Everybody knows the guy who wears shorts all year long. He's a big lug. A rough exterior, teddy bear of a guy. No sleet, snow, or freezing rain can force this macho tower of perspiration from putting on a pair of season-appropriate pantalones. So what if his upper body's outfitted in a parka, ski hat, and turtleneck? Papa's sweaty stems gotta breathe!

Then there's the other shorts-all-year-guy. He's not wearing shorts because his thyroid is out of whack; he's got a different agenda. God forbid somebody doesn't see those horrendous calf implants adorned with the crappy ink he spent his kid's child support money on. He makes sure that even if it's twenty-below, everybody's going to know how "hardcore" he is with his tribal tattoo that looks like leftover bathroom tile from a *Property Brothers* episode. Meanwhile, there's nothing tribal about him. The closest he's come to any Cherokee Nation is popping into the local Jeep dealership on a lazy Saturday. And what better vehicle to show off those gams than a car without doors?

YOU'RE So VaNiTy PLaTe,

I Bet You Think THiS RAnt

is AbouT You

Vanity plates are the cartoonish breast implants of cars. They're a billboard that says, "My personality isn't enough! Do you like me now?" I've never seen one and thought, *Wow! How can I meet this confidently clever Casanova who thought to put 'CYAL8R' on his beamer? Once that light turns green, I'll never be able to catch up with my dreamboat.*

Many vanity plates deserve mocking, but when someone puts the type of car they drive on the plate, that's a special kind of douche right there. VETTE; MINI; BEAMER; HUMMER. Obviously, I know you're driving a Corvette because you practically ran me into the guardrail (and because you have feathered hair and a mustache) when you drove ninety miles per hour to get to that red light before I did. I didn't need it spelled out. It's not like I was thinking, *Geez, was that asshole driving a Corvette or a Nissan Cube?*

Then you have the vomitous couple combo plate. You know some paranoid psycho forced her henpecked man to go along with JANDAN on a moss green Ford Escape that they bought courtesy of the fishing boat she made him sell. God forbid anybody on the freeway thinks Dan is single with his sexy dad hat and sweaty forehead. I saw one that said PATPAT. Are they both Pat, or are they telling me what they do to themselves while driving? Couldn't we all use a little PATPAT after a lonely, late-night, four-hour car ride?

I don't get the plates that tell you their job. If I see INVSTR, am I supposed to honk my horn and shout out my account number so you can make me rich? Or maybe I should just put my account number on my plate and hope INVSTR sees it. And how about the plates that give you advice. Thank goodness I got stuck behind the HAVEFUN gal. I was about to start my day with a domestic dispute, but now I'll start a conga line at work instead because some flake in a VW bug told me to. I wish everybody with a custom plate would just EFFOFF.

61

Psycho Tits Teigen

I never got why Chrissy Teigen was famous but I enjoyed the show *Lip Sync Battle*, so I tried to give her a chance. I thought maybe I was being mean for thinking she was an annoying tool who was trying way too hard to exhibit what she imagined to be a goofball personality. But it turns out my instincts were right. She is a disturbed meanie with decent boobs.

She was exposed in May of 2021 for bullying several individuals online. One victim was Courtney Stodden, who was only sixteen years old when Teigen repeatedly harassed them for marrying a fifty-one-year-old man. Teigen publicly tweeted that she wished Stodden would take a "dirt nap" and privately messaged Stodden to tell them she wished they would die and that they should kill themself. Interestingly, Teigen never wished the same for Doug Hutchison, **the man who groomed and abused** Stodden, or **the parents who didn't protect the teen.** Teigen's apology eventually morphed into a self-pity party and attempts at sympathy for *her* depression and *her* isolation. If anybody should be sorry, it's Hollywood for shoving her down our throats for the last decade and John Legend for procreating with a heartless, insecure crackpot who looks like she could be his sister. #Creepy.

She's been using her excessive "mommy juice" consumption, and her miscarriage, as her get-out-of-jail-free card to say whatever she wants and to troll whoever she wants online. But #TimesUp . . . or is it? It seems the clock doesn't tick for certain people, while others are branded forever—and for much less disturbing behavior.

Hey Chrissy, all of me can't stand all of you.

PaRt 7

I Be MiffEd, BOTheREd, aNd BeWilldereD

People Who Hate the Word "Hate"

I hate to say it, but I hate people who hate the word "hate." Have you ever been to a gathering when somebody comments that they hate something, and then some guy named Bruce in a cardigan clutching a wine spritzer pipes in, "Hate is such a strong word"? Uh yeah, that's why we use it. Like, "I hate Bruce. He's such a wishy-washy, goody-goody killjoy. Who invited him anyway? Probably someone else I hate." Maybe if somebody had used the word "hate" when inviting Bruce (*Fuck Bruce. We hate him*) instead of being nice (*I know Bruce can be a dud, but he means well*), we wouldn't be in this uncomfortable situation.

CeLebRiTy CoupLe NicKNames

Thank goodness J-Rod is over! That was the couple combo name given to Jennifer Lopez and Alex Rodriguez by entertainment reporters. Not to be confused with J-Ro, which is just Jackie Chan saying *J-Lo*. I'm not sure when the couples' nickname trend started, but can it please stop? I'm also not sure what's more annoying: the names themselves or the exuberance in which they're delivered. I can't be the only person who wants to throw darts at Mario Lopez's dimples when he gleefully reports news about Kimye. He looks like he ejaculates glitter every time he gets to say one of these stupid names.

One of the first celeb couple nicknames I remember is Bennifer. Interestingly, this one also included Jennifer Lopez. Hmm, I'm starting to see a pattern here. Anyhow, that was the moniker referring to her relationship with Ben Affleck. Once they split, it was recycled with a 2.0 tag for his relationship with Jennifer Garner. They've since divorced and it's been recycled once again for his rekindled romance with Lopez. Maybe they should change it to Beenifer-there-done-that. Or how about J-Loads? If you ever watch shows like *Entertainment Tonight* or *Access Hollywood*, you're familiar with the happy desperation on reporters' faces when they keep us in the know. When Kat Hoover used to say Brangelina, she looked more satisfied than a 300-pound dude who just pooped for the first time in two weeks. Is this woman getting laid, or does she just roll up copies of the *Enquirer* and go to town on her Vagalina?

It also seems that if a couple gets nicknamed, the name lasts longer than the relationship.

TAKE A LOOK AT THESE DEFUNCT COUPLES:

Tay-Squared = Taylor Swift/Taylor Lautner

Zanessa = Zac Efron/Vanessa Hudgens

Cruise-Control = Tom Cruise/Penelope Cruz

TomKat = Tom Cruise/Katie Holmes

Sayonara = Tom Cruise/Suri Cruise
    (not a nickname; just what he said to her when she was seven)

64

BUZZ(KiLL)WORdS

I hate buzzwords. I even hate the word *buzzword*. They're just trendy words and phrases that get used to death—kind of like Leonardo DiCaprio's penis on a party yacht. As annoying as they are, they're an excellent way to detect people you don't want to empower (buzzword alert!) with conversation. This list primarily focuses on those that, if you hear them being spoken, you know a lot of finger-wagging and head bobbing will accompany them.

CLAP BACK: "Nicki Minaj claps back at Wendy Williams for bringing up her husband's sex offender history." Her ass cheeks also clap back whenever she farts or sways her hips.

FIERCE: This can be used in various contexts, including any reality show on Bravo that regularly uses the phrase, "Bitch, yasss!" But it becomes a buzzword when it refers to a woman accomplishing an otherwise "manly" feat. E.g., "In this month's edition of *Gearhead Today*, we're featuring two fierce women who are breaking down barriers by wearing coveralls to work!" Wow! So you're telling me these trailblazers repair Trailblazers?

GASLIGHTING: A fancy way to describe psychopathic behavior on a reality show full of losers in love. Gaslighting is supposedly used to make one question their sanity because apparently, banging strangers on a reality show isn't enough of an indicator.

GIRL SQUAD: Girl squads are just a bunch of broads with hair extensions and fake eyelashes who all look alike while blabbering on about the importance of being the "real" you despite posting air-brushed (more like heavily painted) selfies and injecting wacky shit into their faces to keep their inner hatred at bay.

HATER: If your friend is obsessed with Kevin James and tries to shove him down your throat (even though he won't fit because his ego's allegedly larger than his belly), she'll call you a hater when you resist.

> ME: "I don't like how he treats people."
>
> FRIEND: "You're such a hater!"
>
> ME: "You're right. Now I hate you too for being so annoying."

HATING: "Bitch don't be hating cuz you man be conversatin' wit' me." No, I'm just hating because you say conversating.

HERSTORY: It's history that takes a lot longer to tell and never seems to get to the point.

IF YOU CAN'T HANDLE ME: ... at my worst, you don't deserve my best. Usually spoken by people in relationships who expect their partner to accept every time they lose their marbles over big deal stuff like: "WHAT DO YOU MEAN YOU FORGOT TO GET MY DRESSING ON THE SIDE!" You know, serious stuff like that.

LIFE HACKS: "Twenty Life Hacks to Make Your Life Easier." Hmm, can number one be to stop making longer words or phrases for perfectly good ones that already exist? 1) Start saying *idea* instead of *life hack.*

LIVING MY BEST LIFE: Putting a hashtag in front of it doesn't hide the fact that you're a douche on a jet ski bragging about it on Instagram. "#livingmybestlife in the Bahamas. Wish you were here, broskis!" Well, maybe you wouldn't be on vacation alone, and your bros would be there if you weren't such a showoff. Even though this phrase is supposed to promote positivity about one's choices, it somehow morphed into a vehicle to narrate every little thing a person or their pet does without a shirt on. "

MY JOURNEY: *My Journey* used to just be a possessive obsession with a great band. I was Steve Perry's number one fan. So as far as I was concerned, they were *my* Journey! The only other journeys I knew of were folks traveling from one place to another. But everything's a fucking journey nowadays: My journey to stardom; my journey to sobriety; my journey to speaking out; my journey to the bathroom at the Mexican restaurant #itsgotime. I blame Oprah for this one. I don't even know if she started it, but it seems like something she'd say and something that every house-hen with Kohl's-cash in her pocketbook would mimic.

[INSERT WORD] + SHAMING: If you're overweight and wear a thong to a public sporting event while twerking and squatting like you're trying to give birth from your ass, anybody who isn't on board is body-shaming. If you criticize a single mom for going through men more often than she goes through diapers for her kids, you're slut-shaming. I can't think of any more shaming examples. I feel so stupid. Oh wait, there you go: dumb-shaming.

LIVING MY TRUTH: How can you live anyone's truth but your own? Unless you're a professional identity thief, you're living your truth. Even if you're a pathological liar, you're living your truth because that's who you are—a fucked up fibber. I'd love to live Lars Ulrich's truth because he's a joyful, kickass drummer with a great sense of humor. But no matter how hard I try, I'm stuck living the truth of an uncoordinated, frizzy-haired weirdo who makes dance videos with her cats (adorably named Hall and Oates, FYI), who doesn't know how to play the drums she's had for ten years.

TOXIC: Chemicals are toxic. People are assholes. You're an asshole if you describe people as toxic. And your asshole might be toxic if you think fried zucchini counts as a veggie.

TRIGGER/TRIGGERED: Adult babies are triggered by words, birds, looks, books, faces, places, planes, trains, and automobiles. They can't function without being coddled but might be triggered if they're cuddled.

WOKE: Another word ruined by white people. You may be woke to racial justice issues, but you're still sleeping at your home in Whiteyville.

SAFE SPACE: If I wasn't fierce enough to clap back but had a nickel for every time someone tried to gaslight me with body-shaming, I could build a safe space to hide from my toxic haters.

65

GROUP STufF

I hate groups—group gatherings, group chats, group texts, group sex, Groupon. They all require much more work than I'm willing to put in. Why do I need that many people for anything other than a "We Are the World" revival? The worst is a group chat about getting a group together to use that Groupon for the new restaurant that serves grouper. I'd rather be a groupie who has group sex with a supergroup (specifically one that includes John Taylor or Mike Ness).

Group gatherings blow. There's always one person who's extra loud and obnoxious, so you're forced to focus on them. At first, you might try to contribute. But why bother? If you can't bulldoze your way through conversations, and you have no plans to hump a keg for hoots and hollers, then keep your trap shut. This attention-seeker is like the mourner who wears a white titty dress to a funeral. I don't care how poignant the eulogy is. The only thing you're focused on are those bereaved boobies. It's the same thing at a gathering. Maybe you're all there for dinner or games. But there's that one dude who always talks like he's got a built-in bullhorn in his throat. Does extra volume mean extra funny? Only if forty-year-old frat boy adds in a tabletop twerk for the group! Bottom line: don't try to compete. Your attempts will be drowned out by loud-guy leading the gang into an R.E.M. singalong accompanied by preppy dancing. You'll be the only white person aware of the fact that you can't—and shouldn't—dance to R.E.M.

Where do I begin with group chats? They stress me out. They're like emergencies. You need to tend to them right away, or you risk dying ignored and alone. Hurry up and get that meme of mommy with a glass of wine not taking any shit from her crotch-gremlins (AKA kids she can't stand) before it's on to the next forty subjects! You have to be rapid-fire with your responses and quips. But how can you when eighteen people in the thread talk about twenty different things at once? You want to care because they're nice people. But you don't care because who gives a shit about whether you put red sauce or powdered sugar on fried dough? Does this warrant an all-day thread of baking-foible and kitchen-disaster GIFs?

I'm part of a couple of online groups that I have no business being in. The people are lovely. They're tightknit. They understand each other. I want to participate, but when I do, it's like I'm the gal that suddenly yelled, *Four inches is fine!* in the middle of a PTA meeting. Everybody stops what they're doing, looks at me, and then carries on without a remark. In their defense, maybe they're being polite because they think I have Tourette's.

But there's a lot of pressure to be part of the group message. And if you can't—or don't—participate several times a day, you're treated like a dude with his dick in his hand at the park. Everybody's hurriedly trying to get out of there without making eye contact. I understand everybody has busy schedules, but besides work, I'm dealing with chronic health conditions that make me feel like five of the seven dwarves on most days. So when I finally have a moment to catch up, I don't always have the energy to chat. If I'm going to get carpal tunnel, it will be from fervently petting my kitty, not from totally appropriate group conversations. Most of the time, I feel lost and left out anyhow, so it reminds me of why I've always been more of a lone wolf. Maybe I should start a new chat group for people who hate groups.

66

The DiRT oN CLeaN ComEdy

There's a view regarding comedy—perpetuated by people who think familial anecdotes are the cutting edge of humor—that only clean jokes can be smart and funny. First of all, *any* joke, whether clean or dirty, can be smart and funny . . . as long as it's written by a Jew. Secondly, I'm not a Jew, but I've been mistaken for one several times (not for my joke writing ability, but for my lack of athletic ability). In addition to touting clean jokes as more intelligent, many also say dirty or edgy jokes are an easy laugh.

How is it easier to get a society full of uptight, personality-censors to laugh at a joke outlining the hypocrisy of religion or politics versus a tired joke about how women are smarter than men? Am I right, ladies? [*Insert image of male comic pandering to females in the audience with a contrived subservient delivery, or a smug housewife comedian with hand extended, palm facing upwards with her other hand firmly planted on hip*]. How is a joke about your wife yelling at you for using the "fancy" towels (*Oh boy, is he in trouble now! What's this silly fella going to say next!*) smarter than a joke that ties childhood obesity into fuel economy? [*RIP Greg Giraldo*].

Meanwhile, the guy who makes the joke about accidentally using the fancy towels almost always implies how he used it to take care of business because the missus won't give him any nookie until he takes the trash out without being reminded. And, uh oh, he forgot to throw it in the hamper and now the dog is chewing on it like a piece of rawhide [*Cheap laughter ensues*]. Somebody's in trouble now Mister! But back to the point of this horrible example. In my opinion, that joke is dirtier and grosser than any joke that might have a "cunt"(the word, not Tobey Maguire) in it. Who wants to envision some slightly overweight, partially balding, super white guy's special sauce? I'm gagging just saying that phrase.

If I work with another self-congratulatory, generic white guy who calls his wife "the sheriff" (if she doesn't have a badge, a mustache, and pull black people over for no reason, she ain't the sheriff), who smirks with delight after "killing" with a set that included a medication side-effect joke and a "kooky" story about his three-year-old, I'll probably take a Viagra, then call Angelina Jolie instead of my doctor [*chuckle chuckle*] and jerk off on the decorative pillows. Similarly, saying something gross or shocking that has no wit to it just for the sake of saying it usually isn't funny either. How many times can we see a blonde, self-proclaimed drunken bimbo talk about how "wrecked" her "pussy" is and act like, "Wow, she is so groundbreaking. I've never heard that sassy, honest talk from a pretty gal before."

I'd rather get a lukewarm reaction making jokes that are real to me than get raucous laughter making jokes that play to the bland simplicity of the majority. I'm not saying that all clean comedy is safe and generic. Jim Gaffigan is a perfect example of a clean, non-edgy comic who is hilarious, original, and clever. And I'm not saying all edgy comedy is unique or revolutionary. What I'm saying is I used to have a crush on Daryl Hall—and although he was a strait-laced singer, it made me feel very dirty inside (that'll teach me for not rinsing that cucumber first).

When I work with clean comics, I don't preach that being politically incorrect is better. I don't toot my own horn (unless I'm really lonely and "accidentally" stumble onto the Mr. Skin website). Yet, frequently, they feel compelled to explain to me how their style is the "right" style and how the bookings are better when you work clean. This usually includes a story about the thousands they make doing cruises and corporate gigs. Somehow, making money while trapped with a bunch of cafones* in flip-flops who refer to a floating buffet as classy is not my idea of making it (but working in mildew-smelling basements or mirrored banquet rooms is). I also have no desire to tell lighthearted jokes about the crazy drivers in [insert your city name here!] before Stan gives his presentation on the benefits of presentations.

I don't dislike clean comedy. I dislike clean comics that think they're on a higher plane . . . and make jokes about planes. It's all about being funny regardless of what your style is. Don't think you're better than someone else because you didn't have any sexual inferences in your act. I don't think I'm better than you because I did. If you're regularly giving unsolicited advice, maybe it's not because you're trying to convince somebody else that you're right; perhaps it's because you're trying to convince yourself you are.

*Cafone (pronounced ga-vone) is an Italian word describing
 a classless, uncouth, or boorish individual

Nosy Neighbors

Nosy neighbors are like HPV infections: everybody has them, nobody wants them, and they always make your partner question your fidelity. Don't get me wrong. I've been known to bust out my binoculars every now and again, but that was only to verify critical information (*Does that broad across the street have a full bush under her arms, or am I imagining it? Is that the same blond he banged last week, or did she grow six inches . . . in the chest? What the fuck is a pergola?*).

But for the love of Godzilla, we don't need to be involved. Be nosy from afar. If you want to know who's pulling into my driveway, have at it. Just don't knock on my door, stop me for "just a quick sec" when I'm lugging groceries, or ask me to sign a get-well card every time Brett down the street falls down and busts his knee. He's an alcoholic for fuck's sake. At least that's what you told me the last time you cornered me.

"WE'RE PrEGNaNt!"

We're pregnant? Uh, I don't think so. Unless "we're" also going to have morning sickness, a torn taint, and boobs that look like deflated animal balloons, you're not pregnant, buddy. *She's* pregnant, and you have a mangina if you say, "We're pregnant!" That saying also begs the question: How did a dick-less dweeb manage to get someone pregnant? If I ended up with a man who was capable of saying *we're pregnant*, I'd do everything possible to avoid that becoming an actual possibility.

This Email

I know this book is about things that I hate, but I don't hate the following email as much as I'm intrigued by it. The author is an accomplished comic and writer who, oddly enough, had lots of typos in his email announcement (which I took the liberty of cleaning up). I changed names and some details (in other words, I made it slightly more interesting and mostly unidentifiable), but it still blows. I'll include my commentary after the email. Enjoy!

I am pumped to announce that the winner of the annual Robin Stite-Slott Award for Best Newcomer in Stand-up Comedy is Hugh Jasole.

The $500 prize was named after my feisty grandma, who loved scotch and vinyl records. She raised me because my mom became a missionary. I guess it was more important to take care of the world's kids than her own. But I loved my gruff grandma. If it wasn't for her sass and no-nonsense approach to life, I wouldn't be where I am today. In her house, Johnny Carson was king, so she was over the moon when I decided to pursue a career in comedy. Whenever Carlin was on, we both felt uncomfortable with his brand of humor. That's when I knew I could prove to my gram I could be a wholesome comedian. Not only have I done that, but I've also vowed to help others with the same ethics.

These values shine through in Buster Hyman. Hyman hails from the nether regions of Long Island, New York. He's hilarious and a regular on the independent comedy scene. He's a social media wiz who you don't want to get into a meme war with—especially if it involves *Game of Thrones*! He relocated to Manhattan two years ago to remain close to his family and friends, and he works as a restaurant host to pay the bills.

Buster's story is inspiring for many reasons. Not only does he have to deal with testy tourists at a busy New York eatery during the day and going to open mics at night, but he also battles cluster headaches. His sense of humor and resilience are what make him a perfect recipient for this award.

Where do I begin? I'm just amazed at how dramatic the writer is about rather ordinary things. Don't most people work to pay the bills? Don't many people live in places to stay close to both family and work? What makes this recipient so "resilient"? He gets painful headaches and somehow manages to tell jokes. Whoa, let's get an EZ-Pass to heaven for this modern-day Harriet Tubman. Imagine the bravery of talking about dating mishaps in front of twenty people while your head is pounding. That's almost as heroic as the yentas who give up gossiping for lent.

Don't get me wrong, I know those are painful headaches because I've experienced similar ones (for chrissakes, I'm pretty sure I get the same kind, especially after an artery spontaneously dissected in my neck and gave me a blood clot). But resilient seems like an awfully strong word to describe a guy with a non-life-threatening condition that can be managed with Advil, swearing, and ice packs. Resilient seems more applicable to a guy who lost his limbs in combat and turns around and becomes the basketball coach for his kid's team. Another utterly random example of resilience is going to school and feeling like a foreigner in your native country because nobody wants to play with you because they've never seen a girl with a mustache before. Add in being impolitely reminded of how bony you are every time you change for gym class, and being told you're too "ethnic" looking to date because most of the Fair Isle McFellas in your town would rather date girls who look like their sisters. And once you escape that disaster, you start working, and although you excel at every job you get, you're continually harassed by old, fat, white men who tell you, "It's the men who deserve to get ahead" when they pass you over for the promotion you were promised, and miserable women who are so vicious you have to end up suing one company after two female managers conspire to falsify your client files in an attempt to make you look incompetent. Eventually, you venture into comedy but you don't fit into any cliques there just like every other area of your life, mainly because you can't explain to self-absorbed assholes that you can't "hang out" after shows because you literally feel like you're going to collapse from the simple exertion of speaking for forty-five minutes, yet you keep on going at it as a lone wolf even when you're debilitated from the undiagnosed illness that turns out to be a genetic disease plus a rare cancer, but you don't want to let anybody down so you continue to care for a terminally ill friend while attempting to mentor and save a suicidal substance-addicted friend even though you can barely lift your arms to wash your brittle hair. That's not a cluster headache; that's a cluster fuck. Again, that's just an entirely hypothetical, random example.

I checked the award recipient out online, and he is hilarious. On top of that, he did an interview where he seems like a super nice guy with a good head on his shoulders (or, in his case, a good headache on his shoulders). So, I raise a glass to the award recipient but an eyebrow to the award giver. Maybe next year's award will go to a guy with hammertoe who resiliently delivers mail by day and punch-lines by night.

WORd TUrdS

I hate that I hate this, but mispronouncing and misusing certain words or phrases drives me nuts. I'm not talking about words like onomatopoeia (I can barely spell that, let alone say it) or anesthetized (which you will feel after reading this). I'm talking about common words and phrases we use in everyday life. I start to cringe when people purposely talk like morons. Or is it Mormons? Or are those one and the same (or are Scientologists morons? Or are they religious terrorists? Wait, what was this rant about?) I also cringe when condescending "educated" people toss out an *alls* or an *irregardless*, not because of the error itself, but because they're unaware of their mistake, so I can't revel in their embarrassment.

Let me be clear. I don't hate the people who use some of the examples I'm about to share. I'm sure I have annoying and/or misused words and sayings that others have politely ignored. In my early twenties, I remember I thought I was so cool for referring to somebody as being *diluted*. When my coworker laughed and said, "Don't you mean *deluded*," I tried to act like he was the idiot instead of admitting my stupidity. I must've been deluded to think he would've fallen for that nonsense. But certain word gaffes make my antenna go up when I hear them, you know? (That's a filler I use that annoys me, yet I can't seem to break the habit!) So let's get to it!

Why does every interviewee on the news say, "I seen" instead of "I saw" when recounting a story? "I seen him in the car." "I seen the way she looked at me." How come they've never seen a dictionary? It makes my skin crawl and makes me want to punch them in the garbled-grammar mouth (and when they report the assault, they can say, "I seen a fist coming at me"). The same people who "seen" are also the ones who "drug." No, I don't mean drug as in a substance; I mean drug as a past tense verb (e.g., "I seen when he drug her body into the woods." "She drug the container across the floor"). Maybe I need to drug myself, so I can speak the same lingo.

———

Following is a list of my most hated misspoken words and phrases in no particular order:

MISSPOKEN	CORRECT
Re-pour	Rapport (Ruh-port)

You can have a good rapport with coworkers, but may need to re-pour if you spill a drink on them. And they may file a ruh-port if you get too close.

Alls	All
Heighth	Height
Reeluhtor	Realtor
Exspeshly	Especially
Worldwind	Whirlwind
Wheel Barrel	Wheelbarrow
I Could Care Less	I Couldn't Care Less
Tooken	Taken

What's the name of that movie Liam Neeson starred in?
HINT: *you've tooken too much time if you didn't come up with Taken.*

All of the Sudden	All of a Sudden
Chipolltay	Chipotle
All Timer's	Alzheimer's
Acrossed	Across
I Seen	I've Seen or I Saw

MISSPOKEN	CORRECT
Got No	Have Any
Ax	Ask
Irregardless	Regardless

Because so many people have misused the word for so long, it has bullied it's way into the dictionary with the caveat that "... a definition is not an endorsement of a word's use" according to merriam-webster.com. Irregardless, it's annoying.

Drug	Dragged
Expresso	Espresso
On Accident	By Accident
It Don't Matter	It Doesn't Matter
Pet a Stool	Pedestal

Even if you make an adorable poop, you should never pet a stool, but you should be put on a pedestal for producing such high-quality feces.

Valentime's Day	Valentine's Day
Sal-mun	Salmon

Don't pronounce the L and don't eat farm-raised!

For All Intensive Purposes	For All Intents and Purposes
Sure Burt	Sherbet

Would I love to go for a tasty frozen treat? Sure Burt, I'd love to have some sherbet with you.

I Resonate with That	That Resonates with Me
Self-depreciate	Self-deprecate
Should/Would/Could Of	Should've, Would've/Could've

I also hate dropping the letter *g* off of words ending in *i-n-g* (even though I'm guilty of doin' it!). I hate using the word *nothing* when it should be *anything*, and the word *like* as like a like adjective and like a filler like, you know? I hate the phrases *not for nothin'*, and *at the end of the day*. How about mid-afternoon? Are the facts different at 9:27 a.m. versus 7:56 p.m.? Another useless thought is *it is what it is*. It can't be what it isn't, so why are we stating the obvious?

In conclusion, I ain't gonna ax what no one thinks of this, ekspeshly people I ain't never seen, because I could care less. For all intensive purposes, let's just say it is what it is. At the end of the day, alls you have to do is like figure out like who you're going to like walk acrossed the street and grab that expresso with on Valentime's Day—and it don't matter who's buyin'. Maybe I shouldn't of tooken such a hard stance on this, but it's not like I drug you here and made you read this. Irregardless, I hope my thoughts took you to new heighths and that you resonate with this.

Daylight SAViNgs

I hate turning the clocks back in the fall. Do I really need to explain this, or are you one of those "it's good for the crops" people who have never even shucked corn, and the closest you've come to cropping is cutting an old pair of jeans into capris? And I know it's a myth that it has to do with farmers, but I wanted a reason to say "shuck corn." Wasn't it God who said, "Let there be light past six p.m. so you can cook on the grill well into winter"? I'm pretty sure that's a direct quote. So let's end the falling back since there's nobody there to catch us when the darkness makes some of us fall into seasonal depression.

YOU CaN'T Ring My BeLL

I feel like I'm in a horror movie whenever somebody knocks on my door or rings the bell. If you haven't seen Sebastian Maniscalco's bit about this topic, I highly recommend watching it. I don't understand why a person would open the door to potential murder, rape, maiming, or worst of all, casual conversation with neighbors! If I'm not expecting you, don't expect me to answer. I'll hide on the floor, behind a door, or in a closet until you get the hell away from my house. I don't like interacting with people I know, so why the hell would I want to open the door for anybody else? And even if I do know you, I'm not opening the door if I didn't invite you. Nothing is that pressing that I have to wipe the Cheetos dust off my chin or put pants on for. Get some manners and leave me to my *Temptation Island* marathon in peace.

Get The FUCK Out of My DMs

Don't misunderstand me. Some decent people send innocent, friendly messages. I enjoy those people. The DMs I'm talking about are usually from clueless creeps and busybody know-it-alls. Here are some things you shouldn't say or do in messages to strangers.

"YOUR TOES LOOK YUMMY" What am I supposed to do with this? Am I supposed to pack my bags and hightail it to wherever this pervy keyboard lothario lays his snapback hat?

"WHERE DO YOU LIVE?" The question is, where do you live as in, what planet are you from to think I'm going to readily provide my where-abouts to a dude who's profile has his education listed as the School of Hard Knocks and whose occupation is listed as "entreepanewer"? If it's not in my profile, for fuck's sake, why would I give it up to an illiterate crack dealer? A well-read one is a different story, of course.

"PLEASE SHARE THIS . . . " Absolutely! Of course, I'll disseminate cockamamie theories and advice from a used car salesman/pod-caster/self-anointed health advisor-legal expert who's fucked in a hot tub. It makes sense that only intelligent people would readily hit the share button, right? [insert sarcastic eye roll here]

"THAT JOKE COULD BE SHORTER" Unsolicited advice is annoying enough, but getting it, in a private message, from some blowhard dickbag you've never met in person is worthy of finally meeting in person just so you can kick them in the back while they're peeing at a urinal. First of all, why are you taking the time to rework my com-edy bits? If you don't get it, I'm not obligated to change it for every basic dolt who only understands outdated impressions of dead (or almost dead) actors, and wife jokes. And secondly, why would I accept guidance from a middle-aged man, who isn't a superhero or rock star, that thinks mutton chops are a good look and who periodically "threatens" people that he'll unfollow them for not interacting enough with his posts? Here's some unsolicited advice: get a life.

"WANT TO GO TO PANAMA CITY WITH ME?" Does this guy really think my only opportunity to get to America's taint is if a creepy computer-stranger lobs an offer at me? Oh yes, please! There are so many appealing things about this invitation; where do I begin? For starters, I have no idea who the fuck you are. I already know you're a low-standard nutcase who's okay with a woman who'd willingly travel with a stranger. Assuming that a person is single—and apparently, desperate—rather than asking first, is ballsy in a scary way, not in a hot way. The fact that your profile picture looks like it was taken from a Google Earth drone isn't helping either.

UNSOLICITED PUBE PHOTOS Here's some advice for every guy who thinks social media is a hookup app. If somebody hasn't revealed their relationship status, location, or nipples, they're probably trying to keep those things private. Being publicly responsive to comments and joking around isn't a veiled request for a shirtless pic of you in a truck stop bathroom with your pubes climbing out of your jeans like Boston ivy.

"HELLO. I'M PRINCE [*insert the foreign name you can't pronounce here*] **FROM** [*insert foreign location you can't pronounce and never heard of here*]. You're no prince to me if you didn't write "Purple Rain" and didn't date Vanity, Susanna Hoffs, or Carmen Electra. Get the fuck out of my DMs.

PART 8

JUST GROSS

Tittoo

The tittoo is a mystical creature made of ink, damaged skin, and bad choices. It doesn't discriminate which tit it lands on—left; right; uni-boob, it doesn't matter. It all depends on the incoherent, haphazard decision-making of the tit owner entering the tattoo parlor at three in the morning. At least that's how I imagine it happening because how else can one explain getting a tit tattoo on purpose? I'm pretty sure there isn't any image or saying that you couldn't have just embroidered on a pillow instead of memorializing it on a slab of sun-damaged flesh.

I've never seen a tittoo and thought, "Wow! I wish I thought of that!" I never slapped myself in the forehead with regret for failing to conjure up a fire-breathing owl skull with diamond eyes to rest atop my boob. And trust me, with boobs as small as mine, I could use any extra advertising to draw attention to this unpopular region of my body. But no. Just no. What's the shelf life of a Jack-Daniels-induced, misspelled, inspirational quote and ugly flower on a boob anyhow? Maybe ten years tops? Most boobs can't survive childbirth or aging, so why remind people of it with your praying hands and misspelled *What wood Jesus do* inscription? Well, I certainly hope we don't need to read her vagina tattoo to find out. I don't want to have to write about a twattoo.

SKaNk YoU VeRy MUCh

As I write this rant, Twitter is in a frenzy over Kendall Jenner's response to a tweet about her being passed around between NBA players (after reports linked her to Devin Booker). Her response contained the word *cooch*. Need I say more? No, I needn't, but I will. She said, "They act like I'm not in full control of where I throw this cooch." Um, gross. Who "throws" their "cooch"? How do you even throw a cooch? Who says *cooch* other than people with less than fifteen teeth and those who've been in a brawl that ended with a clump of hair in their hand?

I can envision her trying to compose that response, ". . . not in control of my love life." *Nah. Too vanilla. How about,* ". . . not in control of my body"? *Nope. That's too evolved. Maybe,* ". . . control of where I throw this cooch." *Ding, ding, ding! We have a winner! This will make momager Kris proud!*

Remember when talking like a skank was reserved for hardcore porn or tricking a guy into thinking you were fun until he proposed? Now it's not only mainstream but it's applauded by legions of people who live their lives emulating Lil Wayne lyrics. People talking all casually on social media about the moisture level of their lady parts, or the various ways they're going to destroy a said person's anal cavity, or how that "D" got them walking bowlegged after the previous evening's Tinder encounter. I'd be embarrassed to admit I wore the same socks two days in a row, never mind give a verbal blueprint of my "cooch" and all its coos to millions of people.

But looking like a porn star and acting like you're in a 24/7 rap video is now the norm. Certain people see this approach to life as being real. Feminists—and the magazines aimed at them—also hold this behavior in high esteem. *Elle* praised Jenner for her cooch comment saying, "she had the perfect response to a sexist joke about her NBA player dating history." Really? There were no other responses that could top that unpolished, turd-covered gem? *Glamour* said, "Kendall Jenner just clapped back at a gross troll who joked about her dating history." She may have clapped back, but the only gross thing was her reply. It's hard to say you slammed somebody when your response was really an insult to yourself. Instead of tossing her twat, catapulting her cooch, or whatever she's doing with that Jenner Jambalaya, she'd come off a lot classier if she'd just zip her lips—both sets.

76

HoaRders WiThoUt BoRders

If you haven't watched the show *Hoarders*, heed my warning: You will become addicted and end up hoarding episodes in your streaming history. You will become a *Hoarders* hoarder.

I couldn't fall asleep the other night, so when I stumbled upon a *Hoarders* episode, I thought, "this will help me fall asleep." Um, not quite. Six hours and six episodes later, I was stuck like glue to the TV (kind of the way important papers from the eighties, take-out containers, and suicidal flies are stuck like glue to a hoarder's walls and floors). You wonder *why* I was sucked in; *why* I couldn't shut the TV off? Imagine a six-foot-tall bearded guy decked out in a terrycloth sweatband (I know, I really don't need to say much after sweatband), a sleeveless khaki vest-shirt, and short-shorts who still manages to look like a biker says, "I have one too many rats." How do you say, "Well, I think I'm going to hit the hay now."

First of all, isn't one rat one too many rats? This guy had (drum-roll please) **over 2,000 rats**! The best part was that these rats didn't emerge and multiply due to his hoarding; these were the *essence of* his hoarding. He kept them as pets. They were in the walls, on the floor, on the counter; they were everywhere (just like God . . . except he doesn't leave excrement on bedspreads).

If you're not familiar with the show, they always send out a psychologist (along with a cleaning crew and professional organizer) to help the hoarder. Every time the psychologist would speak to this guy about the rats, he would let out this kooky-sounding yelp and start sobbing. And the craziest part of it, he was one of the more together hoarders of the series. He didn't fit the hoarder mold (usually, part of the hoarder mold *is* mold). He appeared to have all his teeth, didn't have a waddle to his gait, and wasn't combative. He was cooperative and immediately acknowledged he had a problem. It usually doesn't go that smoothly.

Enter Hanna, my favorite hoarder of all time. It wasn't her hoarding style that wooed me; it was her down-home, old-fashioned abusive charm. Add in a mush-mouth, a walker powered by two of the most flabtastic arms I've ever seen, and a crippled goat, and you have the inspiration behind the saying "what the fuck?" When her daughter tries rationalizing, she explodes like a stifled fart on a first date by pushing her into the wall. Nobody's going to tell Hanna which crusty coupons from defunct stores and smelly pee-stained office supplies she can keep. As she stated, "I'm a cotton picker, ridge runner, stump jumper, and damn proud of it. I don't throw away anything that I can use later." That second statement is astonishing. Not because of what she said, but because she actually used proper grammar putting an *anything* where I was expecting a *nothin'*.

These people never think they have a problem either. They all say the same thing: "I am not a hoarder; I'm a collector." Really? I wonder how much brittle cat feces and unpaid electric bills with Tang stains go for on eBay. Do you think it's a problem when you've "collected" yourself out of your own home and into an unheated trailer that doubles as a chicken coop? Nah, of course not—that's completely normal—especially when all the chickens have scoliosis from being cramped in cages like day-laborers in Toyota Celicas.

I hate it when it's time to get to the "clean-up," and they allow the hoarder to sift through each item ONE BY ONE. Judging by the FedEx box doubling as a poopy pail and the jugs of tinkle in each room, I'm pretty sure you could throw out their toilet, and they wouldn't miss it. It's kind of hard to miss something you haven't seen since Barry Manilow had his original face. When you have so much crap that you have to walk through your home like a SWAT team sneaking up on a meth lab, chances are you don't have a detailed inventory list of your so-called items. If you do have an inventory list, what are the chances you could find it anyhow?

Here are a few tips to figure out if you're a hoarder:

- You have to rake your house
- The only pathway in your house requires you to launch yourself from the top of the staircase to get to it
- Your dining room table is also your curio cabinet, file cabinet, and the cat's litter box
- Your knickknacks consist of Precious Moments figurines, miniature teapots, cobwebs, and mice carcasses
- The only garbage can in your house *is* your house

So next time you find yourself debating whether or not to throw out an expired bottle of Brioschi because you "might need it someday," realize you are one disability check and two estranged children away from becoming a hoarder.

FLiRTy FAmiLy FeUd

Who would've thought that Richard Dawson mouth-molesting every female contestant on *Family Feud* would be the least cringe-worthy thing associated with the show? It seems like all the questions now have a double entendre that always leads to anal. *Family* and *anal* should never be in the same sentence, or the same room . . . outside of the confines of West Virginia . . . or a private browsing session on your Apple device. Survey Says: Gross!

ImmoRaL HyGieNe

We all know what oral hygiene is. Then again, I wouldn't be writing this if that were true. Everybody has been knocked out by pooper scooper breath at least once in their life. Back in my office days, I worked with a girl who had breath that would get to her desk before she did and hang out long after she went home. Her breath was so bad that it was more pleasant to hang out in the restroom in the aftermath of a Chili's ladies' lunch. When I say her breath smelled like a sewage plant (and that was when I held my nose), I'm being kind. How does somebody make out with that? She was married and eventually became pregnant, so I assume kissing happened somewhere along the way. I could barely be in the same room with her, yet somebody was in her. If it didn't bother him, what the heck did *his* breath smell like? More importantly, if that's what her mouth smelled like, what did her . . . ugh, never mind.

I also had two bosses who were the purveyors of their own halitosis havens. They'd lean over my shoulder to show me something, and I was suddenly enveloped in a vent of warm doody. And to all you coffee drinkers/soda drinkers/smokers/water avoiders/shitty-diet eaters/infrequent tooth-brushers: If people are constantly offering you baby wipes instead of gum, it's because your mouth is the equivalent of a loaded diaper. And sucking a mint and slamming some mouthwash is the equivalent of shitting your brains out and attempting to mask it with Febreze so, don't bother. Now you've just scented the odor rather than eliminated it. Fresh Linen feces isn't a treat.

People with medical conditions excluded, there's a difference between the "oops, I had too much garlic" kind of breath versus people who actually have breath that smells like an animal with loose stools died inside of them. We've all encountered this, but how do we handle it? Do you use the direct approach (put a toilet seat lid over their mouth)? Do you go with the subtle approach (wearing a gas mask every time you're in this person's presence)? Most of us are considerate and think, "I don't want to hurt their feelings." But think of how inconsiderate it is for somebody to forego general hygiene and blow mouth-farts at you every time they breathe? You want to tell them off, but please choose your words wisely. "Eat shit" probably won't work, unless you add: "Oh wait, smells like you already did."

YOUR TWERKING AIN'T WORKING

I hate anything that has the word work in it. And yes, I know *twerk* isn't spelled with an *o*, but if it sounds like work, I'm not a fan. I'm also not a fan of anything that comes off as desperate (including myself at sixteen years old when I thought incessantly crank calling my crush would somehow make him realize how desirable I was). But back to twerking. I know it's technically a dance, but is it really? What skill does it take to squat, spread, and shake your ass cheeks like a dog dragging his ass across the carpet to dislodge a dingleberry? It's about as sexy as a dude doing naked gardening. Nobody needs to see a guy fertilizing his petunias with his "personal" sprinkler head. Sit with that visual for a few minutes. You're welcome.

Baby Sniffers

"Mmm. There's nothing like that new baby smell." Uh, you mean the fragrant bouquet of doody, powder, regurgitated cheerios, and head-sweat? The creepiest is that look of ecstasy when the freaks who claim to like the smell of babies close their eyes while deeply inhaling over an infant's head, declaring how "heavenly" it is punctuated with a lengthy "Mmmmm."

And why do people with babies always want you to smell them? And by "people," I mean white weirdos because no way in hell any black person is going around shoving their babies in strangers' faces or sniffing babies like they're fresh-baked cookies. When whitey parents shove their babies in your face, they're like, "Here. Take a whiff. Isn't she yummy? Couldn't you just eat her up!" Nope, no, I couldn't because I'm not Jeffrey Dahmer, and the only things I sniff are perfume, food, and occasionally my armpits if there's a suspicious odor in the room that seems to be following me. It's even weirder when someone asks to sniff another person's baby. We've all seen it when a coworker on maternity leave brings the baby in to show off to her coworkers. There's always that pillow-knitter who rushes over: "Can I hold her? I love the smell of new babies?" Uh, how new? Are we talking placenta new, or just liquid-yellow-diarrhea new?

If you want to avoid a baby sniffer, you can identify them by some common traits:

- Wisconsin or Dakotan accent
- Thinks Tupperware/Avon/Candle parties are parties

- They wear giant glasses that look like they stepped out of a 1974 Sears catalog
- Hairstyle never past their shoulders (usually mid-neck is the longest if the perm is growing out)
- They have napkins and "décor" for every holiday—including the shitty ones like Arbor Day
- They breastfeed their kid until he's old enough to say, "I'm full."

Hopefully, this will help you sniff out the kooks!

BROTOX

It's bad enough that a significant number of females are walking around with the "Do you smell what the Rock is cooking?" eyebrow from Botox and fillers, but we *expect* women to be willing to risk their lives for vanity since society has bullied us into believing we're worthless and invisible past the age of thirty. You can either inject a toxin into your face to cause partial paralysis (and highlight your hair to convince people *that's* why you look so different), or you can roll the dice and hope a facelift doesn't leave you looking like the Joker. But when dudes inject that crap, it's even creepier.

There's nothing more manly than a guy with a face that looks like a perpetually surprised baby's bottom, am I right, ladies? Something about a guy who doesn't have laugh lines or forehead wrinkles makes me believe he wouldn't be afraid to put a needle in his balls either. And why do these guys' faces always look like they were dipped in melted butter? What is that wet shine they have going on? There's no way that a guy who can't live with crow's feet around his eyes is going to be okay with a scrotum that looks like a sad Shar-Pei. Then again, maybe Shar-Peis wouldn't look so sad if somebody would give them some Botox.

GwyNeTh PaltRoW's VaginA CandLe

Should the words *vagina* and *Goop* ever be in the same sentence? A goopy vagina is the last thing I want to smell when I walk into somebody's house, or anywhere else for that matter. If you're wondering what I'm talking about, Paltrow sells a candle called *This Smells Like My Vagina* on Goop, her lifestyle website. In her mind, this is some type of empowering, feministic statement. In my mind, this warrants an urgent visit to the doctor. And people who are paying $75 for this are crazy. Clearly, the correct price point is $69. Can I sniff out a deal or what?

I Don't Love it When

We're Cruising Together

Trapping yourself on a floating petri dish with a bunch of drooling "foodies" because the unlimited cuisine is "to die for" doesn't sound like a treat to me. And I think it's more likely the food is to die *from* than *for*. But that's only if you don't die from the air conditioner circulating liquid feces through the air. Where else do you ever hear of people coming down with Legionnaires' disease other than on a cruise ship or 1976? Nothing says fun like motion sickness and airborne diseases that you can share with strangers steeping in a hot tub. See you on the poop deck!

Look Ma, No Hands!

(Except When I Cough

and Sneeze Into Them)

If you're over the age of ten, and weren't raised by David and Louise Turpin, and you don't know that it's obscene and vile to cough and sneeze into your hands, your face needs to be on a billboard in your community and neighboring towns, so people know to avoid you. This also applies to people who don't try to contain it at all. I'm amazed at how many people who work with the public behave this way. I expect it from a guy on a subway dressed in a Glad Bag with crayons in his hair arguing with himself. But from my cashier and fellow shoppers at Target? Go fuck yourself, you filthy, germ-spreading, uncouth, oblivious animal.

YOUR KiSS is ON My Shit LisT

Picture it. Sicily, 1952. OK, it wasn't 1952; it was 2016. And it wasn't Sicily; it was wannabe-Italy somewhere in the tristate area. And I'm not Sophia from the *Golden Girls*, but I'm pretty close with a gray wig, giant glasses, and some spunk. Anyhow, I'm getting ready to leave the comedy club, so I go to say goodbye to the manager with a hug, as I always have. Not sure why on this night, after working there so many other times, he mistook goodbye for *Clearly, she wants me. I know she can't resist my boxy 1992 JC Penney sweaters and perpetually tightened, irate lips any longer.* He attempts to plant one on me. I casually turn my head, pretending I didn't even notice. I'm the one in the awkward position, yet I'm trying to make sure *he* doesn't feel embarrassed. And even with my thoughtfulness, poof, I was never booked again.

Those kisses are definitely shit-list-worthy because they're basically play for pay. In that situation, you have a choice to suck it up, suck face, and suck at self-respect; or walk away with some dignity and lots of nausea. But I think it's worse to be with somebody you're really into, and when you finally get to kiss, you feel like your mouth is being attacked by a dirty jacuzzi. Nobody's mouth is naturally this wet, so how do they get it like that right before making out? Is there an overly crowded Planet Fitness with broken air conditioning in their mouth? How does one get their mouth to feel like a vessel of sweaty desperation? And please, don't lick your lips and make them look like two shellacked gummy worms before you go in for a kiss. If your partner slaps on a bib before making out (and they're not into baby role-playing), you're a gross kisser.

Swipe LEft bUT WiPe FRONt to BacK

Sometimes when I'm doing my business on the toilet (you know, harassing bookers, trading stocks, etc.), I wonder *now what?* Thankfully, I have a stash of magazines to get me out of such pinches. I flip through until I find an article or blurb on women's health and am relieved to find these valuable, yet difficult to remember, instructions: wipe front to back. What do ladies do who haven't been lucky enough to stumble upon these words of wisdom? What if they mix up Tinder swiping with tushy wiping? Yikes! *Wipe left? No, no, it's wipe down, stop, drop, and roll, right?*

Are there really adults who need the art of wiping explained to them? You wouldn't smear mud on a freshly mopped floor, would you? For God's sake, use common sense. I'm sick of seeing this little ditty in every health magazine and internet threads about lady stuff. Gals, when it comes to wiping, pull yourself together and keep your legs apart.

Guys Who Wax Below the Slacks

Do you think guys shave their body hair so it won't get caught in their barbwire tattoos? Hairless men creep me out. What's appealing about a man who looks like a glistening six-foot baby with calf implants? When I touch a guy, I don't want him to feel like satin sleepwear. I want his skin to feel like a shoe shine brush or like it endured a mild forest fire. I get it if you're a guy who looks like a tumbleweed when you take off your shirt. Nobody wants a dude who looks like he's wearing a woolly mammoth sweater-vest. In that case, trim it up in the front and get rid of it all on your back. And speaking of the front, keep the wax away from your cock-a-doodle-doo unless you're a guy who says "bruh" every two seconds and has a spoiler on your Honda Civic. Well, shave the cock-a-doodle-do and its support crew, but don't remove everything on the path to Penisville.

So what have we learned? Trim down, tidy up, and let your fur flag fly.

Did YOU EVeR KNoW ThaT

YoU'rE My Hair-O?

he·ro / ˈhirō/ *noun*
a person who is admired or idealized for courage,
outstanding achievements, or noble qualities. "a war hero"

brave / brāv/ *adjective*
ready to face and endure danger or pain; showing courage.
"a brave soldier"

The above definitions are from Oxford Languages. Unfortunately, those definitions are irrelevant on social media. It's been annoying enough over the last several years to hear people say *good for her!* every time a body meant for sweatpants has the "confidence" to wear a pair of leggings that look like a vagina tourniquet. We all supportively cheer and raise our fists in solidarity with this soldier of spandex. But now, thanks to mentally-stunted, fake feminist starlets and their dopey fans, we're calling women like Ashley Graham, Julia Michaels, and Halsey "heroes" for having armpits that look like they have a Texel guinea pig in a headlock.

And according to these dimwits, being brave is posting a selfie without makeup and labeling it #allnatural (Technically, I guess eyelashes transplanted from your pubes is natural). But who needs makeup when you've been tucked, pulled, and filled up? More importantly, why are women attaching *#shero, #femaleempowerment, #inspiretoimpact*, and *#badass* to grooming choices? Then again, *bad ass* might apply in this case if they're feeling "empowered" to neglect that area as well.

Back to the armpits. Unless those misplaced seventies porn bushes can save me from a burning building, there's nothing heroic about those stink traps. If anything, those bristly suckers might *cause* a fire. I wasn't even aware this was a thing again (remember when Julia Roberts did it?). But recently, I've caught a few entertainment headlines using words that should be reserved for people who take serious risks such as frontline workers, people who stand up for the defenseless, and anyone willing to criticize Beyonce (that Beyhive is nuttier than a PayDay candy bar!).

These entertainment outlets and fans of these celebrities call them "brave" and "heroes" for posting a selfie without makeup and letting their body hair grow. Can you imagine the gall of equating that with sacrificing your own safety for that of another's? Picture the scene at the pearly gates. "Out of the way Angela Pierce*! Some shallow shithead with chipmunk cheeks and real-pony hair extensions on TikTok is foregoing eyeliner for a day! Coming through!"

I guess somebody better tell Bette Midler to re-record her big hit with new lyrics:

Did you ever know that you're my hair-o
Now I'm not afraid to be furry
I can grow hair like a Sasquatch
For you are the hair beneath my chin

You know what would be brave? Twerking your way around Qatar in a "Girl Power" t-shirt and yoga pants that make your hooha look like a bowl of machboos.

---

*Angela Pierce is an Ohio woman who chose to step in when she witnessed a police officer being attacked by a man during a traffic stop.

PaRt 9

ThaT's NoT ALL

She WRotE

89

The Death of Eddie Van Halen

I can't relate to people who can take or leave Van Halen or whose hair doesn't automatically feather when "Sinner's Swing" kicks in. The thought of being more excited about Pinot and pocketbooks than concerts and Converse is depressing. A life without VH doesn't seem like much of a life at all to me. Of all the things in this book, this might be the one I hate the most. Eddie Van Halen died on October 6, 2020. It was also the same day part of me died. I had no idea how much his passing would impact me.

I was around ten years old when I discovered two bands that would change my life: AC/DC and Van Halen. I was a tiny, shy, anxious kid who thought something was wrong with me because I didn't connect with or relate to the "regular" kids (in my youth, those were your typical jocks and girls who knew how to French braid their hair). I had nothing against those kids; I just didn't gravitate towards them, nor did they to me. I didn't look like them, act like them, or dress like them, nor did I want to. It was unheard of when I was a kid for a doe-eyed little girl in pigtails to wear black sneakers and baseball shirts with iron-on sayings like, "Help Stamp Out Disco in our Lifetime!" (even though I loved disco and still do). I was forced to wear date-rapist footwear—docksiders and Sporto boots—until I laid my eyes on a pair of clunky black, high-top Nikes with a bold white swoosh.

Around that same time, I also heard "Runnin' with the Devil" for the first time. If memory serves me correctly, I was born male, but then I listened to this song and the rest of *Van Halen*, and it literally blew my balls off. This music woke me up and lit a fire in me that still burns today. I never heard anything like it, and I was hooked. I studied every album produced until *1984*—the last with David Lee Roth (until 2012's *A Different Kind of Truth*). I studied every image and every word printed on the covers and sleeves. I would draw the band's logo on every piece of property I owned including book covers, denim, and my thighs. I also collected as many magazine pictures as I could and plastered them on my wall and notebooks. I never had a crush on any of the guys in the band; I just had this immense love affair with their music and Dave's swag. But now, when I look at the devilish smile on Ed's face in every picture, I can't understand how I didn't have a crush on him.

I never stopped listening to Van Halen. It's hard to describe the feeling that rushes through me when I'm listening to my iPod (yup, I still have one), and "Mean Street" or "D.O.A." pops on. The best way to describe it is like the first time you have sex with someone who makes your heart flutter. But unlike romantic relationships, it always feels like that first time with Van Halen . . . when Ed's thunderous riffs kick in on "Take Your Whiskey Home" or "Atomic Punk," . . . it's a romance that never ends. It always lives up to its promise to keep you fulfilled and interested.

Eddie was in a stratosphere all his own. His humble yet brilliant mind was unmatched. A virtuoso with the ability to still be an "every-man." Every story I've heard from friends and strangers has the same theme: he was kind and unaffected. I'm so grateful to have found him when I did; at such a crucial age for figuring out who you are. Seeing their fashion (which was really just a mish-mosh of no particular style) and their fun-loving silliness really spoke to me. I believe this is why I never cared what anybody thought and why it never even occurred to me to try to dress and act like anybody else. I can't imagine what my life would've been like if I hadn't been exposed to Van Halen. And I regret that for the number of times I saw them live that I never exposed myself to Van Halen (I'm sure they would've gotten a chuckle at the "boy" throwing his training bra on stage).

When the news broke, I wept. I tried to stop myself, but I cried like this man was my husband, father, brother, or close friend. It never dawned on me how I was so used to him being an integral part of my life. I listened to his band almost every day of my life since first hearing them. Now, as a DJ for Monsters of Rock, I play them almost every show to over half a million listeners a day. If I wanted to scare the shit out of my mom, I'd turn on Van Halen. If I was down, I'd turn on some Van Halen. If I wanted to rock out in my kitchen, I'd turn on Van Halen. If I wanted to impress the guy in the car next to me, I'd turn on Van Halen.

Ed's sound is inimitable. His body of work is otherworldly. He has left an indelible imprint in music and in my soul. I had no idea how much his death would affect me because I took for granted how much his life affected me. Bottoms up to the man who made everybody want some.

The Red Shirt, Black Tie Combo

Whether it's barn red, fire engine red, ruby red, crimson, cardinal, or maroon, I hate red button-down shirts, and I despise them with black ties. It's tackier than a Canadian tuxedo. Add a tie clip to that sucker, and you've got yourself a defendant. That's right. The red shirt, black tie, black chinos combo is the catchall white trash uniform for weddings, funerals, job interviews, court dates, and *Family Feud* appearances. Don't get me wrong. At least they're attempting to dress up. But if you're showing up to court in that ensemble, an astute judge and jury can quickly determine bad fashion definitely wasn't your first crime.

You Might Be a Slut...

Not That There's Anything

Wrong With That

One thing I missed out on growing up was a slutty phase. I often wish I could've had that laissez-faire attitude that many others have towards sex. But I'm too obsessed with what people's toenails will look like. Or what if they're over the age of twenty-two and still don't have a box spring? Or what if they have a "Saturdays Are for The Boys" banner? Oh, and that little thing that constantly nags at me: what if they're a psycho?

Nonetheless, I'm jealous of that ability to not care; to not overthink; to not gag at the sight of a surprise third nipple (I know throuples are in, but not for nipples. Would that make it a thripple?). So how do you even know if you're a slut? Some people aren't sure, so here's a checklist. You might be a slut if:

- When the doctor says "open wide and say 'ahh,'" you drop your pants and bend over
- Your idea of safe sex is doing it with the car doors locked
- You think a condiment is a rubber that gives you fresh breath
- Planned Parenthood is your alma mater
- Your vagina's had more visitors than the Grand Canyon (Once in your vagina, they think they're in the Grand Canyon)
- You eat two hot dogs at once . . . on your knees . . . no hands

- You put K-Y on your hot dogs
- You miss your kid's kindergarten graduation because it's the same day as your high school graduation
- You go to a gynecologist who has mirrored ceilings
- You're no longer allowed to kneel at church
- When someone says, "Let's blow this taco stand," you actually do

Here's the guy's checklist. Guys, you might be a slut if:

- You have a penis

If at FIRST YOU DON't SUCCeEd at Murder, Try, TRy Again

I was watching a show on the ID channel where some dude tried to kill his ex-girlfriend's new boyfriend. He had every intention of killing him but he just happened to be clumsy. His misstep is the only reason the victim lived. The case goes to trial and he gets six years.

Attempted murder is the only thing you get rewarded for sucking at. A person is given a break because they lacked either preparation, carefulness, or a certain murderous je ne sais quoi. If anything, shouldn't you be punished for sucking so badly? How great would it have been as a kid if this rationale applied? "Honey, while you were at work, Emily tried to gouge out Sean's eyes with a hot poker but she only got one. I was going to take away her Big Wheel but he's only blind in one eye so I sent her to her room without a snack."

While the logical thinking should be that an attempted murderer is the same as a murderer minus the finesse and accuracy, the justice system treats it as an oopsie-daisy. "Sure he had a 157-page manifesto detailing his plot. And yes, he threatened the victim on many occasions, rented a car the night of the crime, bought a wig, a mustache, absurdly large sunglasses, and an inordinate amount of cleaning supplies, but he botched the entire plan. Isn't the embarrassment punishment enough?" What is an attempted murderer going to learn doing his dime minus four in the clink other than more efficient ways to becoming a successful murderer? Is that what they mean when they say "everybody deserves a second chance"?

SOmeWhERe OVeR tHe RaiNBow, I WaNt To StrANgLE You WitH YoUR UkuLeLE

Is it normal to feel homicidal every time I see a talent show singer with that stupid wide-brimmed Porkpie hat tilted on the back of their head doing a lilted-voice version of "Over the Rainbow" on a ukulele? Anybody who looks like a hipster Starbucks barista who auditions with innocence and wonderment in their eyes while doing a done-to-death version of a song that only six-year-olds and perverts like deserves to be strangled by their ukulele strings.

FRieNds... WiTh VagiNas

If you remember that song "Friends" by Whodini, it had some thought-provoking yet straightforward lyrics (not to be confused with most Katy Perry lyrics, which are also thought-provoking; except those thoughts are *Why am I listening to this inane piece of crap?* I don't feel like a plastic bag, but I'd like to put one over my head after listening to her). "Friends" asks a question about the actual number of friends a person can depend on. I asked myself that question recently, which is why I realize one of the things I hate is friends—not all friends—just some of the ones with vaginas.

Let's say I'm seeing—I mean, "some other gal is seeing"—five different guys at once. She doesn't want the guys to find out about each other, so she has to cover her tracks. She calls her friend and says, "Hey Carol, I told Stanley I'm staying with you this weekend because I don't want him to know I'm seeing Arthur." (Apparently, my fictitious whore is eighty-three years old). Now, a real friend (aka FWP: friend with penis) would say, "No problem. Whatever. Do you think Jennifer Lawrence is fully shaved?" But a chick friend would clench her teeth together while sucking air back with a pained squint and say, "I don't feel comfortable with that." You don't feel comfortable with what? It's not as if someone asked you to headbutt a hamster or go to work wearing an "Incest is Best" t-shirt.

Suddenly this felon-fucking, drug-dealer dating, sloppy-sloshed single mom is concerned with morality issues? She's paraded ne'er do well after ne'er do well into her kid's life without a second thought, yet she acts appalled by your choices that only involve

adults? That makes about as much sense as the Shawn Mendes/
Camila Cabello romance.

I don't know if it's because I've been surrounded by irrational,
histrionic, paranoid, neurotic, jealous, argumentative females all
my life (I guess I could've just shortened that and said "coworkers
at all my jobs") that I feel more relaxed around men. Or maybe it's
because I find burping the alphabet funny. Whatever the reason,
I've realized that when the chips are down, my male friends are
there to help with no questions asked (*the chips* is code for my pants).

If you're the gal who doesn't have many female friends, people assume you're a bitchy, jealous psycho. They never think that
maybe you finally got fed up with being friends with bitchy jealous
psychos. These are the ones who can't wait for you to meet their
new guy, but the second you do, they accuse you of flirting just for
being polite. It doesn't matter how busted-looking the guy is; they
always assume you want him. Um yeah, I'm so attracted to a guy
who looks like Droopy Dog and talks like he's gargling a ball sack.
Can I have him? Please!

Women talk about girl power, sticking together, and a bunch of
other crap they don't mean. You can be the perpetual therapist in
a friendship, but it's incredible how quickly your girlfriend's schedule fills up when you need an ear. If you're perceived at any point
as having it better than your "unlucky no matter how hard I try"
pal, you become as useless as Heidi Klum on *America's Got Talent*. If
two dudes are friends and one of them is on the run after robbing
a bank, not only will the robber's friend be his alibi; he'll go rob a
bank himself just so he can send his buddy enough cash to flee the
country. Guys won't let you down, but women will hang you out to
dry like a confederate flag beach towel draped over a balcony at a
Myrtle Beach roadside motel.

95

PaRKINg SPOT TWats

I don't know what's a bigger tease: When your kid's babysitter shows up wearing short shorts and a tube top or that front row parking space at the grocery store. Don't you hate when you see an open spot in the next row, and you hurriedly make your way over only to realize it's handicap? Well, the space itself isn't handicap. It's not like one line is painted dramatically shorter than the other, or there's a very long sign on a very short post. But it happens all the time. The first rows are handicap spots filled with lopsided vans.

Let's face it, handicap parking is no longer for the decorated war heroes who became disabled fighting for this country or a Joe Exotic employee who has to smoke crack with their feet because they lost their arms tickling a tiger. Now it's considered a handicap to lack the ability to breathe through your nose while eating yourself into sugar shivers and to look like the food pyramid rather than obey it. And what do these people need such convenient parking for anyway? It's not like there are handicap aisles once they get in the store, yet they manage to maneuver their way to the trans-fat aisle like a gazelle on the Discovery channel.

Many people say obesity is a disability—just as they categorize drug or alcohol addiction as a disability. Yet, I'm not aware of parking spaces for alcoholics. Where's the sign of the stick figure with a lampshade on his head taking a leak on a lawn gnome? Or how about a sign depicting a sixty-four-year-old man with a ponytail riding a bike in jeans at midnight?

Apparently, being a mother also qualifies as a disability now. And what better way to ease the pain of this infirmity than to give these fertile fuckheads red carpet parking spots? If you see an empty spot and it's not handicap, chances are it's for "Mother with Child." I had no idea having kids was on par with—oh, I don't know—chemotherapy-induced neuropathy, or how about unsteady gait from MS. You had a kid, so now you feel you've earned exclusive privileges, and you shouldn't have to lug your future douchebag thirty extra feet. Having kids: Ooh, just like losing your limbs and your wits in the Gulf War. Somebody better roll out the red carpet for this womb warrior. Nobody else has ever accomplished this unusual feat. So what if you're "exhausted from being pulled in twenty directions because Greg had to work late and couldn't get Ethan to soccer before picking Kayleigh up from ballet." These ridiculous accommodations just feed into the rampant egocentric entitlement of present day.

Interestingly, I've yet to see a "Dad with Child" parking sign. Isn't that a tad sexist? Aren't the dads the ones running out in the middle of the night for Desitin, pantyliners, pickles, and sponge cake?

"Traditional" handicap parking makes sense. It's for people who are limited in some way and can't freely sashay around the store. They have closer spots because walking is difficult and they need some type of aid going through the store (e.g., oxygen tank, walker, resentful adult child, etc.). What's the logic behind closer spaces for mothers? It's not like there are special aisles closer to the entrance just for them once they get in the store. I see moms dragging their kids all over the store with plenty of vim and vigor and not nearly enough wheezing and waddling to justify their parking privileges. If businesses offer special parking because somebody might be a little stressed, then all possible scenarios should be in play.

Let's start with "Guy with Nagging Wife Parking." He needs a close spot to get in as quickly as possible to escape this Zen-zapping dream-dasher. If moms are treated like heroes for "courageously" carrying a ten to thirty-pound kid around, shouldn't there be a reward for carrying the weight of the world on your shoulders? Can you imagine this sign? It's a drawing of a defeated seventy-something guy, cowering in the fetal position with his hands over his ears and a thought-bubble that says, "Yes dear."

How about those heroin addicts? They seem pretty exhausted, and they must be super stressed worrying about how they're getting their next fix. They need to get in the store ASAP to bamboozle the pharmacist into filling their fraudulent opiate prescription. What would that sign look like? How do you draw a stick figure of a stick figure? Or an outline of a toothless ragamuffin stealing checks from her grandparents?

The scratch-off ticket/bottle return guy has got to be pooped. He's dragging that torn bag with $2.10 worth of returnables across the parking lot with his fatigued ticket-scratching arm. He's so tired most of the time that he doesn't remember to put on a shirt . . . or sunblock. Instead of a sign with a drawing, just simplify it with the words: "Unemployed Parking."

What I'd love to see is the "I Just Had Lunch at a Strip Club" spot. That dude needs to get to that supermarket stall that never has toilet paper really fast before he starts shitting fried clams and glitter in the family van.

The point is, where does it end? Pretty soon, they're going to run out of spaces for normal people. Ha! I'm only kidding. There are no normal people anymore. Problem solved.

ARTie FaRty Had a POLitiCaL PArty aNd aLL the BLoWHardS WeRe TheRE

I hate political parties. Anything affiliated with politics hardly sounds like a party. To me, a party involves great music, fun people, and food that tastes great going in, but wakes me up at three in the morning going out like a chili con queso volcano shooting thorough my colon. Mingling with a bunch of nudniks with US flag pins on their lapels doesn't make me want to boogie down the *Soul Train* line. Imagine if I did? I'd get reprimanded by the left for culturally appropriating dance moves and reprimanded by the right for not loving my own race enough.

I've always been an individual and never subscribed to a flock mentality or safety in numbers. Isn't it funny that the people who carry on the most about the beauty of American independence rarely vote as Independents? I have a hard time aligning with anything or anyone that can be so rigid in their thinking or who thinks "Don't Tread on Me" t-shirts are the height of fashion *and* life lessons.

I know and like people on both sides of the party line—even though some are making it a lot harder to continue liking them. People are much more tolerable when they don't reveal their fear-riddled ire. And there's too much finger-pointing involved in politics. Nobody should be waving fingers that much unless they're listening to "Taking Care of Business" on a loop. Now, that's a party I'd attend!

YOU CaN CaLL Me AL

If I Can CaLL You HonKy

"You Can Call Me Al" has to be the whitest song ever. I envision a group of middle-aged people in Jesus sandals with pasty-white hairy toes and lawn chairs dancing around a fire pit roasting s'mores. You can call me *Al* if I can call you *honky*.

HOWaRd Be Thy NAme

In April 2021, an opinion piece by Maureen Callahan appeared in the *New York Post* bashing Howard Stern. I decided to submit my own opinion on her article, and despite my response not getting published, I decided to include it here. For some reason, certain people who started listening to Stern several years ago are infuriated that at almost seventy years old, he isn't the same guy he was at twenty-two. They lose their shit that he isn't there to babysit them five days a week, fifty-two weeks out of the year. I wonder why they don't harass TV actors for only delivering an average of twenty-two new episodes per year. I understand people have different tastes and enjoy different things, but I don't know why people who don't enjoy a show study it, obsess about it, and create groups/threads/articles to angrily dissect it rather than just stop tuning in to it. That's what healthy people do—they move the fuck on.

I think most people would agree we're all striving to achieve the American Dream. If you search for the definition of the American Dream, you'll find varying descriptions, but they all include references to one achieving their desired success and attaining financial freedom. Imagine if you had financial freedom. Would you say, "Fuck my own happiness. I want to please a bunch of ungrateful assholes instead"? Strangely, that's what the anti-Howard Stern brigade expects. Here's the response that I sent to the *Post* that didn't get printed:

I read Maureen Callahan's April 27, 2021 opinion piece, "Howard's End: Shock Jock Stern has lost his sting—and His Mojo," and it made me cringe.

I've listened to *The Howard Stern Show* since the Jackie Martling days. I say that only to clarify I'm not a newbie or somebody who used to listen. I listen every day (yes, all three of them) from start to finish. And while I'm a fan and devotee, that doesn't mean I agree with one-hundred percent of everything Howard says. In fact, I think that's what makes me the best kind of lover—accepting the person you love despite your differences. When the positives far outweigh the negatives, it's a relationship worth keeping. I can survive one too many Jennifer Witz impressions if it means I also get to hear Sal and Richard prank calling *Tradio*, or Howard ragging on Gary's throat clearing affliction.

The article opens with a lie, stating that the *Stern Show*, "long in decline, is dead." There was no data such as ratings or financials from his employer to back up her assertion. I think it's safe to say that it wouldn't bring in any revenue for SiriusXM if the show were dead. If it's not making the company any money, it would've been a perfect time not to renew Howard's contract. Instead, he inked another multi-million-dollar, five-year deal. Either SiriusXM needs a new bookkeeper (maybe they can hire Callahan), or they know why a significant number of people are subscribing. Howard is the only reason I still have SiriusXM.

The next dig in the article refers to Stern having "fled to his basement" when the city went into lockdown in 2020. I'm not sure why this is supposed to upset supposed fans. Most of us "fled" to basements, kitchens, spare bedrooms, or wherever else we could do our jobs from home when the pandemic started. I do a morning radio show, and I was working from my closet for a while! I'm not ashamed of it, and the fans still got the content they were accustomed to. My best friend works for a cable television network that still has most employees working from home.

Callahan surmises that Howard has no intention of returning to the studio despite being vaccinated and returning from "yet another vacation." If this woman is a true listener, she'd understand satire, sarcasm, exaggeration, self-deprecation, and bluntness. Anybody who's a fan knows part of what makes Howard funny is his neuroses and his perpetual panic over things that might be insignificant to others (scary that a pandemic would be trivial to others, but that's a different op-ed piece). She takes his comments about not believing the pandemic will ever be over as a literal statement rather than an observational one based on extrapolatory information such as the continued selfish behaviors of many Americans. Without getting a majority on board (read about how New Zealand did it), it's not unreasonable to be frustrated and exaggerate your conclusions . . . for a COMEDY show.

The writer also seemed upset over Howard having "yet another vacation." I hear this complaint a lot from other "fans" as well. The anger that people seem to have over something any of us would snatch up if given a chance is mind-boggling. The man has been doing this for over forty years. If he wanted to do a show one week per year and somebody wanted to pay him for it, that's his right. I'm sure that if any plumber, accountant, store clerk, or other worker's company said, "Hey, we want to give you three months off a year," they'd all be okay with it. The fact that Callahan, or anybody else, would feel anything but indifference about another person's vacation is almost disturbing. If anything, I'm excited when Howard's off for a week because I know I can get more of my own work done since I won't be glued to the show.

Now here's the part that really got me: "Stern, 67, renewed his contract with SiriusXM last December, signing for five years at a reported $120 million per year. This is incredible, considering he works three days a week, Monday through Wednesday, broadcasting maybe three hours per day, about 112 shows per year with 253 days off." The show being on three days per week rather than five has long been a source of ire for many fans. It's hard for me to even call them fans when fans are people who are supposed to root for you, kind of like friends. If my buddy told me his employer said he only had to work three days a week without a change to his salary, I'd be happy for him. And if I had an agent who could negotiate a deal like that, I certainly wouldn't fire him. But if you're a true fan, maybe you'd have some insight into other possibilities on how the reduced schedule came to be.

Robin Quivers beat a cancer that she wasn't supposed to have survived. None of us know what her specific status is now. Some cancer patients remain on maintenance chemo for the rest of their lives. Some have lifelong complications and side effects from the treatments they've endured. It's entirely possible that five days a week was no longer a viable option for Quivers. Whether it was done to accommodate Robin or simply because they damn well earned it, it's nobody's business but theirs. And it's also a possible reason that Robin doesn't do the news anymore (something Callahan also criticized without insight or a thought as to other conceivable reasons). The best part of the news was how it ended up dragging on for an extra hour (sometimes longer) with Howard's add-ins, unexpected guests, and Fred's brilliant sound effects. Maybe Robin knows her physical limits these days and knows she can't pull it off with the 110% she always had. Just because the audience isn't privy to the reason doesn't mean there isn't one.

The worst part of the op-ed was when Callahan states, "Indeed, Stern sounds like a guy who should have retired years ago, one begging to be fired, an attempt to end his own misery. Howard: Your

listeners are right there with you. Put us all out of your misery."
She acts as if she's a prisoner to a show she seemingly despises.
She's paying for a radio service and can't summon the strength to
switch to another station? That doesn't seem like a great emotional
or financial decision. She bitterly describes the "Groundhog Day-
like" show, sexed-up Ronnie, and Howard's "much younger model
wife Beth . . . and the hundreds of rescue cats that cycle in and out
of their house." Wow, what a terrible thing to help animals in need
[insert disgusted eyeroll here]. To throw that in as if it's terrible to
help animals makes me question what she thinks should happen
to these cats. Should they also be "put out of their misery"? Yikes.

She also seems irritated, like most former fans, by Howard's
evolution as a human being. I hear people say things like, "The old
Stern wouldn't say that." Or, "The show ain't the same no more."
Well, I certainly hope that by the time I reach my sixties, I'm not the
same nincompoop I was in my twenties. I know I said and did things
in my younger years without understanding some of it. I'm grateful
that my core has always been based on empathy and compassion,
but that doesn't mean I always did things perfectly. To expect never
to have new thoughts or ideas in one's lifetime is a narrow, ignorant
approach to oneself.

It's also ignorant to believe somebody should rail on a friend's
wife just because you have a radio show. We all get that Hilaria
Baldwin is a kooky asshole for pretending to be from Spain. That's
creepier than when Madonna adopted a British accent. But if he's
a friend with the woman's husband, Alec Baldwin, it would be out
of line to insult his wife just to get some laughs on his show. We
all have friends whose partners we can't stand. Do we go publicly
mock them? Of course not. Out of respect for your friendship, you
just privately make fun of them with other friends. I'm more upset

with Howard for being friends with Baldwin, a staunch supporter of Woody Allen.

After a critique of Stern's leaked ranting at a meeting, Callahan suggests he can't get any A-listers on the show. So, Bradley Cooper, Lady Gaga, Miley Cyrus, Chris Rock, Metallica, Charlize Theron, Brian Cranston, and Paul McCartney aren't A-listers? That might be news to them. As a lifelong fan of the show, I actually get more enjoyment from the staff nonsense and internal goings-on, so whether he gets big names or not is of no interest to me.

Her final (attempted) slam quotes Stern as saying, "Sirius has treated us in a very odd way. We're gonna fix that. I've heard [SiriusXM president and CCO] Scott Greenstein say, 'Oh, why would we put [Artist X] on your show?' . . . What are you, f—king high? You put them on our show because we're the only channel anyone's listening to." To this, Callahan ends her piece by writing, "Not anymore." I think this was supposed to be her metaphorical mic drop, except the entire article proves that she *does* listen, fervently—desperate to find anything to criticize, perhaps in retaliation for something he may have criticized on-air that doesn't align with her own beliefs or behaviors. It's not time for the *Stern Show* to go away to appease people who can't grasp commentary or humor beyond Sybian rides. It's time for people who are confused or threatened by change to learn how to change the channel.

Hey Diddle Diddle

Josh Duggar

Roman Polanski

Jeffrey Epstein

Ghislaine Maxwell

Prince Andrew

R. Kelly

Jeffrey Jones

Michael Jackson

Gary Glitter

Bill Hutchison

Paula Poundstone

Ian Watkins

Jerry Sandusky

Jared from Subway

Jon Schillaci

Oliver Francis O' Grady

Jerry Lee Lewis

Remy Gonzales

Jimmy Savile

Jim Watkins

Reverend Richard Bucci

Vincent Magera

Seán Fortune

Stephen Collins

Doug Hutchison

David Berg

Dr. George Reardon

A. Joseph Maskell

Victor Arden Barnard

Earl Bradley

Larry Nassar

Richard Huckle

Mark Salling

The UNfUCKables

Meth Heads. Granted, we'd probably save a lot on toothpaste and dental floss, but I'm already sleep-deprived. I can't deal with a dude wearing pants belted under his ass cheeks with coat buttons for earrings who's awake for ninety-six hours straight.

Guys who wear mandals or flip-flops.

Soda Drinkers. Once in a while, soda is fine. But you're not a six-year-old at a Chuck E. Cheese birthday party. So, grow the fuck up and drink some water.

The Property Line Obsessed Guy. We get it. You lack inches elsewhere, so you freak out when they're taken from your lawn too. Calm the hell down and go drink a Schlitz in your mossy-oak-camo recliner.

The Not-for-Nothin' Guy. I can't help but envision this guy using bread as a ladle for soup, gravy, or sauce while frenetically shoveling it in his face like a gorilla. Not for nothin', but what a friggin' cafone.

Karens. Stop spewing what you believe is medical, legal, or constitutional jargon to intimidate people trying not to die at work, walk their dog in a park, or enter their own apartment despite not being white. You know nothing. You are nothing. You sound like somebody in a roid-rage tirade minus the athletic ability, but with all the stupidity. Nobody has to put up with this unstable day-drinker expelling verbal feces all over the joint.

The Cardiologist Who Told Me I Needed a Psychiatrist. Years later, I was diagnosed correctly (but only after an artery in my neck spontaneously dissected and caused a blood clot). Even though I would never fuck him, he certainly fucked me. Thanks, lazy Dr. Douchebag.

Women who have ever uttered the words, "I'll fight for my man!" "Don't fuck with my man," or anything of the sort. If that's her approach, doesn't that make her more of the man? If you have to maim his side pieces and bully him into being faithful, maybe you should fight for better comprehension skills. He's letting you know exactly where you stand; so no amount of threatening or reprimanding is going to make him want you.

Plastic Surgery Face and Plastic Celebrities Who Plug "All-Natural" Beauty Products. Okie dokie Christie Brinkley, at almost seventy, your face is immobilized from rolling a wand over it. Shove it up your ass! Actually, it looks like a vibrator, so you know where to shove it.

Anyone Who Says "It's Wine O'Clock!" Do you know what else time it is? It's time to eat a piece of shut-up pie, you annoying suburban mommy.

Women Who Have Vocal Fry and Make *Statemennnts* that Sound Like *Questionnns*?

The Ironic Mustache Guy. You can have a sense of humor; just not on your face, please.

Reese Witherspoon. "Don't you know who I am!" Remember that hissy fit when she was pulled over for drunk driving? Yes, we do know who you are: a phony, spoiled, out-of-touch twat who should buy Christie Brinkley's face wand to shave down your chin and your ego.

The Person Driving with One Leg Up. *Aren't I the coolest with my laid-back approach to operating a piece of heavy machinery without a care in the world?* You're driving a car, not in a Kumbaya circle at a spiritual retreat, you irresponsible ignoramus.

Long Fingernail Guy and Super Long Fingernail Gal. If a guy doesn't make time to do something as simple as trimming his finger-nails, I can only imagine what other basics he doesn't have time for, like wiping. Or worse yet, he does wipe, and his long finger-nails trap all the debris. And what's up with the women with those freaky long nails that come to a point in the middle? If you don't scratch furniture, chase mice, or bathe with your tongue, lose the claws before you put your eye out trying to apply those trashy eyelashes that look like broom bristles.

The TV Talent Show Audition Hat. Wearing a hat that makes you look like you're walking around in an enormous, fabric picture frame doesn't make you an artist or unique. It makes you North Dakotan.

The Person with the Stuffed Animals in Their Rear Car Window. You need attention. From children. We're creeped out. Buh bye.

Double Standard Guy (DSG). DSG is the guy who can't find enough women to put his polluted penis in. No matter if he's at a PTA meeting, a bar, or his mom's funeral, he'll bang any chick willing and able (okay, sometimes neither willing nor able), then calls them a whore afterwards. Despite being a "whore" himself, he seems to think he's a great catch (maybe if you're trying to catch crotch crabs) and that it's okay to insult women for doing the same thing he's doing.

The Half-Moon of Hair in the Back with the Ten-Inch Clump of Hair Swooped over the Front Guy. We all know this guy is some type of perv—usually a pedophile with outlandishly large, square-framed tinted glasses, or a family man, known as a pillar of the community, who frequents prostitutes on the nights he's "attending a men's-only bible study group." And why do these guys always drive a '94 Cutlass Supreme? Is there an abundance of them on the For Sale page of 8chan?

Anybody Who Got Their Knickers in a Knot over this Book. Laughter is the best medicine. The ability to laugh at yourself is therapeutic. So instead of getting pissed over a joke you chose to be offended by, be pissed at yourself for taking stuff so seriously and wanting to turn every difference of opinion into a crazed dad-screaming-obscenities-at-the-little-league-coach kind of a moment. If I hear a joke I don't like, I simply don't laugh, and I don't think about it again. If you're the person who takes the time to tweet, post, write letters, send messages, or start a campaign over something you found unfunny or you recognized yourself in, can you please say a prayer for me when you go to hit the reset button at church on Sunday? Thanks. #forgiveness

And

ANOTheR

Thing...

The Best of the Rest

- The state trooper/military haircut

- The word gubernatorial

- The joke about the closet space on every episode of *House Hunters* (she gets the walk-in; he gets a corner on a shelf)

- Homeschooling and everything else enjoyed by people who've never cut their hair (but have bangs for some reason)

- B&Bs

- Whispering

- Water-Saver Toilets (water isn't saved if I have to flush five extra times just to part ways with Meatloaf Monday. Case closed.)

- Destination weddings (obnoxious, rude, and entitled)

- Sunday weddings

- Weekday weddings

- Morning weddings

- Long weddings (any ceremony over ten minutes that doesn't include an Elvis impersonator singing "Burning Love" is just self-indulgent)

- Fitted wedding gowns

- The "children should be seen and not heard" people

- Frat brats

- The people who say "he hasn't paid his dues"—as if they know every detail of a person's life and what they've done or been through.

- Fake feminists

- Diarrhea

- Name hogs. Anyone who thinks they own the rights to a child's name and gets pissed when a friend or family member chooses the same name can't be fun, can they?

- People who say they don't watch TV. We know you don't because you're boring, you drink soup from a mug, and cram commentary on local budget cuts into every conversation.

- Poprah Winfrey disciples

- Sammy Hagar constantly badmouthing David Lee Roth. It's not a good look and neither are his mom-from-the-Midwest-capris and curly bob.

- When you pick up your pizza and they put the cold salad on top of the hot box

- Family update letters. Update: No one gives a crap

- People who rustle rappers at the movies

- People who refer to themselves as blessed

- People who don't return a smile or a wave

- ASMR videos

- Hilaria Baldwin's fake Spanish accent

- Indian food. I'm not racist.

- People who say, "We really needed it" when it rains. Unless you're a farmer, shut the hell up.

- My editor not allowing me to spell *mustache* with the *o* (e.g. *moustache*)

- My original book designer who told me "done is better than perfect." A book with misaligned text and fucked up formatting isn't done; it's giving up. Maybe give up drinking when you're working? Just a thought . . .

100 Things I Love

This list isn't all-inclusive since I can't list everything I love. It's in no particular order and excludes obvious things like family (not all family—there are definitely some stinkers in the bunch), friends, pizza, and Betty White. I love:

1. The Heat Miser

2. Greg Giraldo

3. Only-in-Florida stories

4. Old people farting in stores

5. My homemade dark chocolate bark

6. Drunk dads falling down trying to dance at weddings

7. Reality dating shows that I'm too old to watch

8. Humility and courtesy

9. Sour Shoes' impressions of Baba Booey and Chris Mad Dog Russo (especially when he says "hullabaloo")

10. Chris Mad Dog Russo

11. Sunny days, warm weather, and the beach

12. My niece's hilarious impressions of family members including the one she does of me getting my picture taken (I call it the awkward-trying-to-be-sincere smile)

13. Animals (especially rescued ones)

14. Anyone who can breakdance

15. Fresh fruits and vegetables

16. Playing drums (I can't, but I keep trying)

17. Watching people talk without their dentures

18. Naturally round derrieres (I just wanted to say *derriere*)

19. Cheese (the sharper and smellier, the better)

20. Gentlemen

21. Flirty Gary

22. *Burning Love* (but not burning genitals after some love)

23. People-watching

24. Awkward Family Photos (the website, the calendar, and the game)

25. People who can laugh at themselves

26. Sal Governale's "My Wife" and "Photograph" song parodies

27. Sal Governale and Richard Christy's prank calls to *Tradio* and *Swap Shop*

28. People clapping off beat

29. When people pronounce *Italian* as *eye-talian*

30. The episode of *Frasier* when he goes into the gay bar, Bad Billy's, wearing Niles' squash shorts after his ripped.

31. My homemade sauce and meatballs

32. People of Walmart website

33. Dressing up

34. Leslie Nielsen in *Naked Gun* and *Airplane!*

35. Apple pie, apple crisp, and apple turnovers

36. Pale pink peonies and Dinnerplate dahlias

37. Hall and Oates (my cats and the greatest duo in music history)

38. When Hall drags his wand with the jingle bell and feather boa on it down the stairs and drops it at my feet to let me know he's ready to play (my cat, not Daryl Hall. That would be cool if he did that, though!)

39. When Oates rolls over for me to rub his belly (my cat, not John Oates. That would also be cool . . . or weird . . . I'm not sure)

40. Music (rock genres including classic, hard, punk, metal, and hardcore; R&B, soul, ska, Motown, Sinatra, swing, yacht rock, eighties new wave, eighties new romantic, corny seventies and eighties love songs, a few random country songs, some pop, a few boy-band songs, and whatever else makes my socks go up and down)

41. Dancing

42. Robin Quivers' singing

43. Kids; especially with glasses

44. *Curb Your Enthusiasm*, especially any episode with Marty Funkhouser

45. People with balls who aren't afraid to stand up for what's right even if it means going against "the group" they belong to and being called a traitor (Integrity is brave and hot. Blind loyalty is pathetic and weak)

46. Natural boobs—whether they look like bologna loaves or sausage patties—as long as they're real, I'm a fan

47. Saying *Bananarama* with a British accent

48. When Australian people say, "G'day mate!"

49. Classic movies like *Charade*, *The Tender Trap*, and *Gentlemen Prefer Blondes*

50. Five o'clock shadows on men (not so much on women)

51. People who understand sarcasm and satire

52. Toned arms

53. Barfly bodies (linebacker chest with giant tits, no waistline, and super skinny legs)

54. Finding that hair on my chin to pluck before I go out in public

55. *Nobody* (the bus scene is killer!)

56. One-hit wonders

57. Sour cream

58. The Jerky Boys/Johnny Brennan

59. Summer concerts

60. Steve Harvey's reactions to his own jokes

61. Autobiographies and memoirs by musicians, comedians, and mobsters. I highly recommend Nick Culmer's *We Don't Serve Your Kind 'Ere*

62. Converse sneakers

63. Men who aren't afraid to cry (when it's appropriate . . . not when they see a spider)

64. Black church (it seems way more uplifting and less depressing than honky church)

65. Interior decorating

66. Seeing couples fight in public over inconsequential things

67. *Impractical Jokers*

68. Loving parents

69. The face Oates makes after "mistakenly" sniffing Hall's rear end (again, my cats, not the musical duo . . . as far as I know)

70. Late seventies/early eighties Yankees (Nettles, Guidry, Rivers, Winfield, Jackson, Dent, Piniella, Randolph, Gossage, Righetti, etc.)

71. Mid-nineties Yankees (Rivera, Williams, Posada, O'Neill, Matsui, Jeter, Martinez, Pettitte, etc.)

72. Road trips

73. When Peter crashed his car listening to "Panama" on *Family Guy*

74. Belting out "And I Am Telling You I'm Not Going" by Jennifer Holliday with my friend, T-Bone

75. Brainteasers, puzzles, crosswords, word jumbles, and word scrambles

76. Low-rise jeans (when will this high-waisted-mom-jeans trend end!)

77. All episodes of *Bewitched* involving Larry Tate (even with the crappy replacement Darrin)

78. *Fast Times at Ridgemont High*

79. Bea Arthur as Dorothy on *Golden Girls*

80. *The Carol Burnett Show* (Harvey Korman ruled!)

81. Walking in the rain

82. People who just get it (and you don't have to explain what *it* is)

83. *Archie*, *Sabrina the Teenage Witch*, and *Josie and the Pussycats* comic books

84. The fact that I didn't even know I was my best friend's beard for over twenty years (I knew he was gay. He didn't know I knew. I didn't know he told everybody I was his girlfriend. I cracked up when he told me.)

85. Tommy Heinsohn (I'm not a Celtics fan but he was my favorite sports commentator)

86. Having my back and arms tickled

87. The feel of velvet (when I was about four or five, I slept with my velvet dress so I could pet it)

88. The segment where people slip and fall on *America's Funniest Home Videos*

89. Simply Lays potato chips and Cheetos

90. Roller skating . . . in my kitchen

91. *Mr. D*

92. Joke gifts. I'm an excellent gift-giver, but my joke gifts are even better. Some of my hall-of-famers are pig's feet for a vegetarian, a subscription to a Christian magazine for a non-religious person, a ginger merkin that had to be shipped from Lithuania, and petrified cat feces.

93. Old people. I always enjoyed elderly people. As a teen, we had a pair of elderly sisters as neighbors—Edith and Flo. I enjoyed their company more than most people my age. When I was in my twenties, I was friends with a seventy-eight-year-old woman. We played cards, went to lunch, and laughed a lot. Old people are cool.

94. The rare nights when I actually sleep for more than two hours before waking up again

95. Mad Libs

96. The fun and good-hearted people I interact with on Twitter

97. Flip phones (if mine didn't die in 2019, I'd still have it)

98. Toasted cheese sandwiches preferably on seeded rye bread

99. I don't watch a lot of dramas but these are the ones I am/was all-in on: *Ray Donovan, Godfather of Harlem, City on a Hill, The Shield, Dexter, Breaking Bad, Sopranos, True Detective, Luther, Goliath, You,* and *The Deuce*

100. The reaction I get when people find out I had a pet chimpanzee when I was little (we couldn't have a cat or a dog, but somehow a chimp was okay)

Acknowledgments

I want to thank my mom not only for her insightful feedback and genuine excitement about my book, but for having a sense of humor and letting me watch *High Anxiety* when I was seven. Exposing me to comedy at such a young age and watching comedians like Robert Klein, David Brenner, and George Carlin really awakened the observational jokester in me. Once I got into stand-up, there were a few people who always kept me busy with work without expectations of anything else and were especially kind to me: my buddy Mike McKenna, my concert buddy Jonny Benson (you are gold!), and Jack "Gator" Schuler.

My gratitude to Steve can't adequately be put into words for all the support, honest critiques—even when I didn't like the feedback—and for all the funny ideas that helped unlock my writer's block. Most importantly, thank you for taking on so much stress (but trying to hide it) when my health was at its worst. I can finally say, "I'm dun Miiikuhhllll!!" writing this book, and I couldn't have done it without your help.

Thanks to Dina for some of the outrageously hysterical ideas that made me giggle like a ten-year-old who discovers how to write out boobs on a calculator for the first time. Thank you to Jim for also providing hilarious as hell suggestions as well as for your initial help converting the manuscript back to a raw document after the first designer left me with a diamond dipped in diarrhea. And to Dina and Jim for letting me monopolize many of our walks and group texts with book-talk and providing me with insightful and useful feedback.

I'm so grateful to Scott for being my test audience on many rants and offering assessments and reactions that were not only funny, but also thoughtfully shared. Thanks for being someone I trust implicitly and for being an SPK Literary Ninja. Now you wild out!

Special thanks to Sabrina for always having uplifting, complimentary, and clever things to say that kept me motivated and confident. You have a wonderful way with wittiness and words. And thank you for providing your superior proofreading skills. It meant a lot to have you involved in something so important to me.

I'm so thankful to LiLi, Nick, and Zach for sharing their opinions on the cover photo and design, and to LiLi for taking the time to discuss with me and listen to me about the boring technical aspects of writing and publishing a book. It helped more than you know.

My heartfelt gratitude to T-Bone for always showing a genuine interest in the progress of my book and regularly asking me for updates. I treasure your friendship.

To Ronan (Babe!), John & Eileen, and all of the genuinely kind people I interact with on Twitter (and sometimes Facebook and Instagram): thank you for asking about the book and keeping me inspired.

To Harlan: I can't thank you enough for all of your help. Thank you for having so much faith in my talents. I mean, why wouldn't you? I'm fucking awesome.

Thanks to my pal, Michael, from Keep Rock Alive. He noticed me early on [*stalker much?*] when I first started promoting myself for Monsters of Rock. We clicked right away, and he helped me grow my Twitter following when he dared me to share a video of myself "dancing." He saw something in me [*outside my window through his binoculars*] and always tried to help in any way he could. Grazie my east coast paesano!

Without my cover designer, Laura Duffy, this book wouldn't be "me." You totally took the design idea to another level and finally made this feel like a "real" book! You are incredible and in a league of your own.

I can't put into words the gratitude I have for the most amazing interior design and layout person ever, Karen Minster. Thank God (AKA Laura Duffy) for sending you to me. I had no idea how tedious and complicated this part of the process was. The amount of time, care, and thoughtfulness that you put into making my book look so friggin cool is unbelievable. You saved me after a horrible experience with the first designer, and I gained a beautiful friend along the way. I still expect to have two-hour conversations with you!

And much gratitude to my Twitter buddy, Kirk Johnston, who gave me the idea for the "100 Things I Love" list and for regularly checking on my progress. You're a real pal.

I had this concept and list for many years, but didn't start writing it until I became a chemo partner for my friend Pat (Scott's mom). I had a few hours at each of her treatments to write, and a captive audience to listen to my crazy ideas. If she were still here she'd say, "Good job Baba Ghanoush. How many copies you think you can get me?" (She loved free stuff . . . that she didn't need). I have no idea why she called me Baba Ghanoush, but it cracked me up. She'd also say "Fuck cancer, fuck 2020, and fuck 2021! Now get me a hot dog."

I couldn't release this book without those who showed genuine interest and shared their opinions as I was writing it. But if it bombs, it's partly their fault.

Lightning Source UK Ltd.
Milton Keynes UK
UKHW010417261122
412877UK00013B/233/J